DEEP RESPONSE

An Emergency Education in Post-Consumer Praxis

Tyler Disney

First Edition, 2024.

ISBN 1: 979-8-9922551-0-2

ISBN 2: 979-8-9922551-2-6

ISBN ebook: 979-8-9922551-1-9

www.tylerjdisney.com

For the forum.

Table of Contents

1. You Are Walking Into A Trap

I used to think that climate change, overpopulation, and biospheric degradation were problems. In identifying them as problems, I assumed there were solutions, which kept me from seeing that my way of life had to change.
--Peter Kalmus

I'm standing in the rain on the sidewalk outside of the house I lived in twelve years ago, near Telegraph and 61st Street in Oakland. The old post-war bungalow is as I remember it: tired-looking, layers of paint softening its lines and giving it the illusion of pulling into itself.

I let myself in and open the door to the first room on the right. It's a small bedroom. The mattress pushed into the corner takes up most of the space. Immediately inside the door is a desk piled with books, pads of green graph paper, empty coffee mugs and beer bottles, and a beat up laptop with glowing red keys.

And there I am. There he is. I mean, my twenty-five year-old self is sitting with his feet up on the desk, big over-ear headphones on, a book in his lap. He scowls up at the intrusion and then his face freezes as he recognizes me.

Apparently he was not expecting his thirty-eight year old self to burst into his room tonight.

He pulls the headphones down around his neck and I can hear the music clearly now. It sounds like Wolves in the Throne Room, which seems appropriate.

"Hi," I say. "We need to talk."

He pulls the plug on his headphones and tries to speak but it comes out a croak. He tries again: "What?"

"I'm you, visiting from twenty twenty-four. There are some things I need to tell you about."

He stands and steps right up to me, well inside my comfort zone, and studies my face. I'm oddly okay with it. I suppose it is *our* comfort zone, after all. This is going to be a strange night.

He's got a good ten to fifteen pounds of muscle on me, a remnant of my college powerlifting phase, but he looks softer. I'm leaner and harder now. He could probably beat me in an arm-wrestling match but I know I would outpace him on a long trek in the mountains with a heavy pack.

I watch him study me. He's got my signature scowl, all right. It doesn't mean he's mad, it means he's thinking. His eyes settle on mine and I can see their question: *Is it true? Are you me?* I hold his gaze calmly. His scowl fades to neutral, which is as close as I got back then to expressing surprise.

"Holy shit," he says softly.

I put my hand out and he shakes it reflexively. "It's good to see you again. I know this is a lot, but I need your attention right now. I need all of your attention. So why don't you get any questions out of your system before we dive in."

He blinks at me and opens his mouth but doesn't say anything. He's going to need a moment to get his brain back online. I never was terribly quick on my feet. I walk into the kitchen to give him some space.

"Roommates are out, right?" I call over my shoulder as I start opening cupboards. It's been twelve years, I don't remember where I kept stuff.

"Yeah, they're at a wedding or something."

"Good. They'd probably think this was weird." Ah, there it is. A bottle of rye bourbon whiskey, middle shelf stuff. I grab it, sniff check two small mason jars, and come back to sit on the couch in the living room. My younger self is standing in the doorway to my room now, staring at me.

"You don't have any questions?" I ask.

"What's the future like? You're *time traveling?* How? Is that a normal thing? Did aliens come and give humanity time travel tech, or--"

I hold up my hand to slow him down. Apparently his brain engaged. "Yes, I'm time traveling. No, it isn't typical. Honestly it's a long boring story that isn't relevant. No aliens yet. The future is – we'll get into that, that's central to what I need to talk about. Any other questions?"

He thinks for a second. "Do you have kids?"

"No," I say.

He nods. "I can't think of anything else. Why are you here?"

"I am here," I say, "to discuss the next ten years of your life with you." I hold a jar of bourbon out to him.

He takes it and sits and squints at me.

"Are there, like, killer robots running around in the future that I have to kill the inventor of? A big catastrophe the future needs me to do something to avert?"

"No, nothing that cool. Sorry." I genuinely am sorry. This would be a much simpler conversation. "Almost precisely the opposite, really."

His eyes narrow. "What does that mean?"

I clear my throat and ignore his question. "Tell me about your life."

"My life? You already know about my life. You should tell me about yours."

I wave him off. "I will. It's been twelve years, my memory isn't that good. I want to hear how you think and feel about your life right now. What's going on? What's it like? How are you thinking about your future?"

He sits back and blinks a few times. "Life is good. I'm having a lot of fun. Work is great, I'm getting to work on some really cool projects. And people mostly just leave me alone and let me crank. I don't get micromanaged at all. I spent the winter running around with Occupy Oakland, which was..."

I smile. "…a *lot* of fun. I remember that."

He nods. "I'm single now, which is great. I just finished paying off my student loans so I'm going to be saving up now. I feel really unencumbered. My roommates are great. I feel really free and like I'm on the right path. Seriously, though, why are you here?"

"What do you care about most?" I ask, ignoring his question. He gives me a puzzled look. "What do you care about? What's your purpose? What gets you out of bed in the morning?"

"I care about decarbonizing the built environment in order to mitigate climate catastrophe," he says, "and I care about reducing resource demand to a point where we aren't destroying ecosystems in order to keep our society running. I care about having a built environment that is beautiful and healthy, not ugly and toxic. Everything is designed wrong and I want to help make it better."

"How's that going?" I ask.

"It's going well," he says. "I've been working in the sustainable built environment for three years and it feels like I've just about got my bearings. I'm working on innovative projects with other smart people who share my vision. The company I'm working for only takes worthwhile projects. It's an exciting time."

"And what are your plans for the future?" I ask. "What's your vision for the next five to ten years?"

He eyes me uneasily, sensing that I'm talking him into a trap. He's right. "I want to be an expert at this. All of the projects I work on will be zero net carbon, regenerative, probably Living Building Challenge certified. The firm won't seem so cutting edge because the industry will have begun to catch up, and making beautiful low-resource-consumption buildings will be status quo. I'll be part of that, working to spread the knowledge around the industry. The sense will be that we're making steady progress towards a world that is put together well, a world that sucks less than this one."

"How about your life outside of work?" I ask.

He blinks a few times, looks around the room as if noticing it for the first time, then shrugs. "I don't think I'll be in the city for very long. I like the idea of fixing up a classic trailer, living somewhere close to trailheads in the mountains, and working remotely. Take breaks from work to ride the trails or backpack or climb. That sounds like a solid life I could do for a long time."

I nod. "That's about what I remember. This is a really good year for you."

"Yes, this is a great year," he says. "Especially after the last three."

I nod again and clear my throat. He looks at me. I look at him. He frowns. "What?"

"You fuck it all up," I say.

"What?"

"You are running into a trap," I say. "That's why I'm here. I need to explain the trap to you and tell you how to avoid it."

His eyes dart around the room as if looking for tripwires or thugs lurking in the shadows. "What trap? What are you talking about?"

"You spend the next eight years burning yourself out physically and emotionally. You do work on some cool projects. You will become an expert in a few domains. But in eight years you will feel like the world you want is moving away from you faster than you're moving towards it. You will not feel like you're making steady progress towards a world that is put together well. You will actually be profoundly uncertain if you're doing any good at all. The idea that you might be causing unintentional negative side effects will keep you up at night. You become unconvinced that the strategy you're pursuing is an effective one. You sense that there is something seriously wrong with your understanding of how the world works and you work very, very hard to figure it out. But you don't figure it out.

"Along the way you'll bounce between states of manic, existentially panicked workaholism and lethargic states of despair that anything you're doing matters. You'll sporadically distract yourself with alcohol, dysfunctional relationships, and daydreams that you never do much about. But you aren't wired to numb and look away for long. You keep returning to it, beating your head against the wall.

"On the surface your life will look okay, but under the hood all is not well. The more clear it becomes that your vision of contributing to making the world a better place is not happening, the more you thrash. The more you thrash, the less effective you become. In eight years, despite throwing yourself at professional and personal projects aimed at contributing to the crises facing humanity for most of a decade, you exist in a twilight state between despair that your life will ever mean anything and anger that you're in this position in the first place. In short, you fizzle."

He looks like he just swallowed a cupful of fermented swampwater. I am describing his worst nightmare. "I fizzle," he says. "I don't understand. How?"

"Your fundamental mistake is that you think what's broken is out there," I gesture vaguely at the world outside the walls of his house. "You've correctly identified a large number of technical problems with how society functions. Buildings use too much energy to operate and require too much carbon to build. Too many of the materials used in our built environment are toxic and are poisoning us. Our cities are designed for cars, not humans. You've identified a number of technical solutions to these technical problems: use better design to build buildings out of non-toxic materials, require less energy to operate, and require less carbon to build. Arrange them in a way that makes it feasible to use public transportation, bicycles, and legs. These technical solutions are all well and good, but if the whole world adopted these technical solutions everything would still burn. We'd still wreck the planet.

"You think that since you've identified these technical problems, and can see technical solutions to these problems, and possess the skills necessary to implement those solutions, that you are part of the solution. You aren't. You're part still of the problem."

"What's the solution then?" he asks.

"Realizing that there *is* no problem," I say. He gives me a blank look. "The issue isn't that you can't solve the problem, it's that you're confused about what the real problem even is. This confusion contributes to a lot of dysfunctional behavior in your life. The real problem is that very few people understand the true nature of what we're facing. It seems hopelessly difficult because the technical nature of what appears to be the problem is monstrously complex. No brain could disentangle it or make sense of it."

"So, then, what can I do?" he asks.

"When you find yourself beating your head against a brick wall, try looking to the sides and see if maybe you can just walk around the thing. You're trying to figure out how to make things work within the logic of the system that exists, and it seems impossible. What's one possible obvious explanation for that?"

"Maybe it *is* impossible to make things work within the logic of the system," he says.

I nod. "And it's very popular to *talk* about thinking outside of the system, but almost no one actually does. For the most part people just dress a little differently. They're cargo-culting the revolution. It's actually very, very difficult to undergo a fundamental shift in paradigm. But that's the actual next step."

He shakes his head. "I don't get it. I'm working on decarbonizing the built environment. That's what I actually do 40 to 80 hours a week. And that's basic thermodynamics: we need to be pumping less carbon into the atmosphere or we're hosed. There's no woo-woo paradigm shift that needs to happen, it's just simple physics. Decarbonize or die."

"Yes, but is what you're doing actually decarbonizing the built environment? Or is what you're doing slightly decreasing the life-cycle carbon footprint of expansionary commercial real estate development that is cruising along with the business cycle like it always has? Is your work just another case study of Jevon's Paradox? And when was the last time you felt like one of the buildings you built needed to get built, like it was a critical and valuable addition to the lives of the human and more-than-human world? Convince me, right now, that what you're doing isn't just splashing green paint on the same boring story."

He doesn't say anything because I know he's already begun having his doubts, already begun asking himself these questions. He just doesn't know that he isn't going to find satisfying answers for another eight years.

"What the world needs is not cleverer technological fixes at the same level of thinking that got us in this mess in the first place. What the world needs is fundamentally different thinking. And you are not thinking as fundamentally different as you think you are," I say.

"What do you mean?" he asks.

"Your highest-level criticism of the way society currently runs is that it's using too many resources, right? That it's consuming more resources than the earth can supply on a renewable basis?"

"Yeah, of course," he says.

"And how much debt are you carrying right now?" I ask.

He shifts in his seat and breaks eye contact. "It's just a few thousand, but that's because I just moved and I'm about to pay it—"

"You don't pay it off," I snap. "You carry five figures of credit card debt for most of the next decade. You don't know how to live below your means as an individual, and you think you're qualified to help the world bring its consumption within planetary limits? You talk ecology and thermodynamics but you live debt and overshoot. How could you possibly contribute to the ecological function of the world if you can't pull basic ecological function off at scale of your own life, which you actually have total control over?"

"I don't understand how you go into that much debt and hold it for so long," he says. "That seems deeply uncharacteristic of me."

"That's exactly the problem," I say. "You've got some weird psychological contradictions that cause fundamental dysfunction in the economy of your household system. And you're not that abnormal. Living slightly above one's means is average behavior. What's weird about you is that your values are in stark contrast to your actions, so you live with a heavy load of cognitive dissonance. Even if you did live just below your means instead of just over it, you'd still be far from operating in the space of ecological economy you say you want for the whole world."

"But that's hard," he says. "I mean, society isn't set up to allow that. The modern world is set up for people to live mostly paycheck to paycheck. Housing is insanely expensive. Supply chains are just in time.

The whole thing is set up in an insane way, that's part of what I want to change."

"And this exactly is your error," I say. "You think the first thing you need to do is change the world, and then your personal life will fall in line. You've got it precisely backwards. You're trying to change the world from System A to System B while running System A software in your head. That's impossible. That's like trying to invent an electric car by incrementally making improvements to internal combustion engines. You can make a much more efficient internal combustion engine, but you're not going to make an electric car, ever, with that approach. What you want to do is to contribute to a totally different kind of society, a culture that operates according to totally different rules. But you insist on playing by the old rules in your personal life. That's why you get nowhere."

"So, what do I do, then?" he asks. "What are the new rules?"

Get Your Own House in Order First

"Learn how to live below your means. Develop a broad skill set. Learn how to have functional relationships. Figure out why you're addicted to broken things. Develop resilient systems at the household scale. Internalize systems thinking within your own life. As you develop competence and work with a new paradigm at the personal scale, *then* you can start expanding outwards."

"We don't have time for turning inwards, for being selfish," he says impatiently.

"You're right, we don't have time for that. But we definitely don't have time for arrogant morons running around like they're god's gift to the future just because they've noticed some obvious technical dysfunctions. You're liable to cause more problems than you solve with your level of thinking. You're rushing around in a panic and it isn't justified."

"What do you mean not justified? We have to move fast—things are getting worse, we're racing toward tipping points, ecosystems are in collapse—"

"We ran out of time in the seventies," I snap. "We had a window of opportunity in the seventies. We could have turned this whole thing around then. But we didn't. We abandoned all the work people were doing then and we stomped on the gas pedal in the eighties and nineties. Now we no longer have a problem to solve. We have a predicament to respond to."

"A predicament to respond to?" he asks.

"Problems have solutions," I say. "Being *on a trajectory* towards eventual overshoot is a problem. Reorganizing society and reducing global consumption in a timely manner was a solution for that problem that we did not implement. Being *in* global overshoot of carrying capacity is a predicament. You cannot solve a predicament, you can only respond to it. How we respond to the predicament of overshoot matters a great deal. Pretending that we can 'solve' what we're facing is a categorical error in grasping the reality we now live in.

"Unfolding catastrophe that unravels our infrastructure of industrial logistics is baked into the cake at this point. If we'd stuck to the momentum we built in the seventies we might have been able to glide-path society to an ecological civilization without incurring disruptive tipping points. But that's no longer the situation we're dealing with. We're operating too far above the carrying capacity of the world and our infrastructure can't handle the reversion to sustainable levels of consumption while maintaining cohesion."

Anti-Defeatist

He gapes at me. "You are a defeatist. You become a defeatist. I can't believe it. You're talking about giving up and just trying to have a nice little life in a bunker somewhere—"

I slam my hand on the table between us. "I am not! Don't put words in my mouth. Listen to me. You're so stuck in your narrow vision of being a hero. You don't see that what you're trying to save is the very thing that got us in this mess in the first place. You're trying to hold up something that you should let fall. You don't see that new systems will emerge from the dissolution of the old system, and *those* are the systems that deserve your attention and effort."

"What new systems?" he asks.

"I mean the successor cultures that are emerging from the dissolution of this one," I gesture around us. "Cultures that operate based on rules aligned to biophysical reality. The cultures that are growing in the cracks of the old system.

"You need to understand that you can't work on these successor cultures if you're still running the programming from the old system. If you're still trying to brute force everything and operating in a state of overshoot, unable to think in systems, fragile to disruption, enmeshed in dysfunctional psychological patterns, unable to carve out time to think and respond to the future as it arrives. In a very technical sense of the word, right now you don't *deserve* to work on these new cultures. You will damage them if you try to. This is why you have to collapse your scope to your personal life, to the scale of your household, and build a functional system at *that* scale before you expand back outwards again. You have to become the kind of person who can contribute meaningfully to these successor cultures."

I know this is hard for him to hear. He's got so much effort already invested in his current way of thinking.

"Or," I continue, "you can keep doing what you're doing. Huck yourself at projects, pull overnighters, burn yourself out on projects that get canceled anyway, trash your relationships and your health, and drown in the uncertainty that any of your sacrifice is worth it. Along the way rack up five figures of consumer debt with nothing to show for it at the end. Your call."

He gives me a steady look, and then stands up and goes into his room. He returns a moment later with a notebook and pen and sits back down on the sofa.

"All right," he says. "You have my attention. How do I become this kind of person?"

I smile. "This is what I time traveled twelve years into my past to tell

11

you. This is what it'll take the rest of the night to explain."

Further Reading

Kalmus, Peter. (2017). *Being the Change: Live Well and Spark a Climate Revolution.* New Society Publishers.

Rowson, Jonathan. (2021, February 9). *Tasting the Pickle: Ten flavours of meta-crisis and the appetite for a new civilization.* Perspectiva. https://systems-souls-society.com/tasting-the-pickle-ten-flavours-of-meta-crisis-and-the-appetite-for-a-new-civilisation/

Hagens, Nate. (Host). (2022, October 26). Daniel Schmachtenberger: "Bend not break #4: Modeling the Drivers of the Metacrisis" [Audio podcast episode]. In *The Great Simplification.* https://www.thegreatsimplification.com/episode/42-daniel-schmachtenberger

Greer, John Michael. (2006). *Problems and Predicaments.* The Archdruid Report. https://archdruidmirror.blogspot.com/2017/06/problems-and-predicaments.html

Giampietro, Mario, and Mayumi, Kozo, (2018). *Unraveling the Complexity of the Jevons Paradox: The Link Between Innovation, Efficiency, and Sustainability.* Frontiers in Energy Research, 6. doi: 10.3389/fenrg.2018.00026

2. The Man Who Connected The Dots

The "system," which many of us like to blame our problems on and yet count on for our solutions, is not really governed by a mysterious group referred to as "them." The world that we live in is the aggregate sum of the individual behavior of all of us. "They" are not responsible for our world. We are! Unless you are a dictator… the most effective change starts with individuals using a bottom-up approach. You have to become the change you want to see.
-Jacob Lund Fisker

"Look up Jacob Lund Fisker," I say.

"What?"

"Eff eye ess kay ee arr," I say, miming thumb-typing on a phone.

He does it, reads, scrolls. Reads some more. A gust of wind flexes the window panes. I can hear the screech of the BART train in the distance.

"It should be the first hit," I say. I'm surprised it's taking him so long.

"An astrophysicist?" he asks. "A Danish astrophysicist?"

"That's the guy," I say.

"What does neutron star fluid dynamics have to do with anything? Is the sun going to blow up or something?"

I scowl at him and grab the phone. I don't know why he's being obtuse. Our google-fu has always been strong, and this is an easy one. I look at the search results. It's a mix of Danish and English websites. Some academia.edu stuff, some really esoteric astrophysics stuff, a couple hits from the Oil Drum in 2004 and 2005.

What the hell?

I type in another query. Nothing. Something dark prickles at the back of my head. I type three letters into the search bar. Nothing.

"Oh, no," I breathe.

I tap to the second page of search results. I see an article from 2010 from the San Francisco Chronicle. It's about a yacht race. A yacht race *accident*. Low visibility conditions, collision, freak accident. One sailor lost to the sea: J. Fisker.

"Oh, no," I drop the phone on the table and stare at it. It is a confusing moment for me. If someone you know dies in a parallel universe, does it make sense to mourn for them? To feel grief? My emotional state doesn't have the keenest grasp on my dimensional reality at the moment, so it feels like I've been punched in the gut.

"So, this makes things difficult, this is… *shit*." I get up and walk to the window. Rain ticks against the pane. It sounds to me like a clock running too fast. *There are a million universes where Jacob dies in that race, and a million universes where he doesn't,* I think. *I've landed in a universe where he does. This is why that elder god winked at me when he ported me here. Son of a bitch! I've got to pull myself together. C'mon, brain, c'mon, get back online, I need you right now.*

"The truth is, I didn't figure this all out for myself. I wasn't clever enough. I never connected all of the dots and figured out how to get my life put together right. Someone else connected the dots and I just found his notes. *He* figured it out," I turn and point at the phone. "Jacob wrote a book and started an online community way back in 2010. Two years ago for you. I found his stuff in 2020, and that's what finally got me pointed in the right direction."

I look bleakly at my younger self. "But in your world, in your universe parallel to mine, he dies somewhere over there," I wave vaguely in the direction of the Bay, "before he publishes anything."

"That's… really sad," he says. "But you can still explain it, right?"

14

"This stuff isn't – I was going to come here, tell you to get his book and join the community, and then I was going to walk you through some of the common misconceptions people have when they find his stuff for the first time. He wasn't writing for people like us and so it's easy to think it's just a self-centered strategy. You probably wouldn't pick it off a shelf right now. I was going to make sure you understood the real purpose and power of his work, but *it* was going to do the heavy lifting once I'd left." I'm pacing now.

"I spent years, *years,* trying to figure this stuff out before I found his work, okay? Trying to put it all together. I had most of the pieces of the puzzle but I couldn't figure out how they fit together. *He put them together.* He connected the dots. There's nothing else like it. I've read hundreds of books, I've been to the end of the internet and back, and I haven't found anything else like it. It's genius, I think it's actually genius, okay? I'm not being flippant. And it doesn't exist in your world. And I have to go back to my timeline by dawn. This is a problem."

"You didn't bring a copy with you?" he asks.

"Every gram counts when time traveling," I say, "No room for bringing stuff that should already exist at your destination."

I stop pacing abruptly, spin his journal around towards me and start writing in it.

"What are you—"

"Books," I snap. "In case I have an aneurysm in fifteen minutes or something. You might be able to connect the dots with this list."

I fill one page, flip it, and fill the next. I'm aware of him sitting there uneasily but I ignore him. I draw lines between books and add short notes to the lines.

"Okay," I say and spin the journal back towards him. "Those are puzzle pieces for you to read later. Tonight, I'm going to try to explain the framework, I'm going to try to explain a method for putting the pieces together that will make sense to you."

I do another round of breathing. Three slow in, hold for three, out for three, hold. Where to start? How to not say it in a way that it bounces off of him? There are consequences to saying the right thing in

15

the wrong way.

"Okay. All right. Let's do this."

Further Reading

My alternate-past self can't read Jacob's book, but you can:

Fisker, Jacob Lund, (2010). *Early Retirement Extreme: A Philosophical and Practical Guide to Financial Independence*. Jacob Lund Fisker.

"What is ERE?", accessed August 28, 2023, https://wiki.earlyretirementextreme.com/

"Early Retirement Extreme Forums", accessed August 28, 2023, https://forum.earlyretirementextreme.com/

Robin, Vicki and Dominguez, Joe, (1992). *Your Money or Your Life: Transforming Your Relationships with Money and Achieving Financial Independence*. Penguin Books.

3. To Cope With Unfolding Environment

The most important thing in life is to be free to do things.
--John Boyd

"Why are humans so great?" I ask.

"Huh?"

"How is it that humans came to dominate the planet? If you look at our physical attributes it doesn't make much sense. We can't see in the dark, we run slow, we don't have claws or fangs, we're not very strong, our babies are helpless for years after birth, and we don't even have fur to keep warm. We appear to be weak, slow, sitting ducks. And yet we dominated the planet. How? Why us? Why not wolves or raccoons?"

He holds his hands up and says "Opposable thumbs?"

"Work with me here. Woolly mammoths did well in the ice age, but then they died out. Neanderthals didn't make it. We made it. Other species do fine in their ecological niche, but if that niche changes or you put them somewhere else they don't do well. We spread out to every single continent. If we were a superhero, what would our superpower be? What are we better at than any other species?"

"Oh, you mean how we're generalists. We're not super good at any one thing, we're good at adapting our behavior and tools to whatever environment we find ourselves in."

Humans are Adaptation Machines

"Yes. We're adaptation machines. We adapt cultural and behavioral patterns to environment, which is way faster than genetic adaptation. We adapt culture and technology from the Arctic Circle to the Sahara with the exact same biological hardware. Adaptation is the essence of humanity."

He shrugs. "Yep, that's neat. What does that have to do with anything?"

"How long has the climate been stable?" I ask.

"Oh, I see where you're going with this," he says. "The climate stabilized ten thousand years ago, began the Holocene, and that stability allowed us to spin up things like agriculture and complex hierarchical societies."

"Right," I say. "For quite some time we've been adapting our social systems and tech stacks to a stable climate, which—"

"—which is about to go unstable again, because we just dumped a totally unprecedented amount of greenhouse gasses into the atmosphere," he finishes.

I nod. "And we're running up against other biophysical limits having to do with the carbon cycle, and we're monkeying with every single ecosystem dynamic we can get our hands on, and we're drawing down critical resources like topsoil fertility, and all of these things have an impact on the stability of the bio-physical-social-cultural construct that makes up the human world. Yes. The smart money is very much not on continued stability of the climate or of our global resource distribution systems. But our culture and infrastructure is tuned for a stable environment."

"So, as a species, maybe we've lost our edge when it comes to adaptation," he says. "We've lost the knack of it, because we've been busy adapting to one really stable environmental condition. And we're headed into our greatest adaptation challenge yet in the very near future."

"Right," I say. "We haven't lost the inherent ability to adapt, that's hardwired, but culturally we've gotten unused to it and built a bunch of technological and social systems that are fragile. Have you started reading Boyd? Don't tell me he doesn't exist in your timeline either."

"No, he exists. I started reading him last year."

"What does he say the strategic aim of any organism is?" I say.

"It's to increase freedom-of-action on our own terms."

"There's a little more to it," I say. "Do you remember?"

He shakes his head.

"Grab it, let's find it."

He knows what I mean. He goes into his room—our room?—and emerges with a blue paperback book. He flips through the pages. "Here it is. *'The strategic aim of any organism is to increase freedom-of-action on own terms in order to cope with unfolding environment.'*" He closes the book and looks up at me. "To cope with unfolding environment."

"That's what everything came down to for Boyd," I say. "Winning is successfully coping with unfolding environment. Losing is failing to cope with unfolding environment. The entire spectrum of Boydian strategic thought unfolds from this core insight. Humans coped with the coming of the ice age. Humans coped with the going of the ice age. They coped with moving from Africa to every single other bio-region on the planet. Sometimes environment changed rapidly enough that large swathes of humans died out, but always some number of us hung on, adapting by the skin of our teeth, and we made it through. So. Adaptation is important. Yes?"

"Yes, of course," he says.

"And what do you need in order to adapt, according to Boyd?" I ask.

"Freedom of action. Autonomy."

"And how much freedom of action do you have?" I ask.

He blinks at the abrupt shift from the abstract to the specific. "Uh, a lot?"

"Do you really?"

"I'm pretty free, man. I'm white, male, unattached, educated, physically and mentally healthy. All I need is a small trust fund and family friends at Harvard or McKinsey and I'd have been the poster child of white male privilege."

"Yes, historically speaking you have enormous freedom," I say. "Thank you, liberal democracy and the birth lottery. But you aren't taking advantage of your potential freedom, not barely at all."

"What are you talking about?" he says. "I just spent the winter running around with the Occupy Oakland people while holding down a full time job where I'm working on decarbonizing the built environment. I'm using my privilege to rather full effect, I think. And, I mean, I was able to adapt. That morning when the cops bulldozed the Occupy encampment, and everyone came back at night to try and retake it, that day came out of left field for me. But I had sufficient freedom of action to show up just because I was curious. And then we got tear gassed and somehow that clinched it and I wanted to be involved. We coped with and adapted to unfolding environment to engage in an unpredictable opportunity."

Threats to Freedom

"Could work have restricted your freedom of action?" I ask.

"I guess. Projects could have been insane at the time and I could have been working seventy or eighty hours a week. But it was mellow at the time."

"What about, ah, how to put it… what did the people at work think about your extra-curricular activity? Your boss?"

"The founder of the company honored me at the holiday party for my involvement. He was an anti-nuke activist back in the day, and most other people in the office were at least supportive, so it's not like I had to hide what I was doing. They're all great."

"And what if it'd been different? What if they'd been against it? You and ten thousand others shut the Port of Oakland down for a day. Not everyone was cool with that. Some people thought you and your friends ought to be locked up for sedition."

"True. If people at work hadn't been supportive, that would have been a different thing. I mean, I still would have done it…" he trails off.

"Even if it meant risking your job?" I press.

He's honest enough to think about it. "I think so, but I can't really know, can I? That's not how it was, so I didn't have to make that decision."

"Fair enough," I say. "What would have happened if you had lost your job?"

He shrugs. "I'd have had to get another one."

"How soon?"

"Within a month or two."

I sit back and consider my words. Him talking about Occupy was a lucky break. He made my point for me. I need to make sure he really gets it though.

"You *happened to have* a fair amount of freedom of action at the time to be able to pursue it. You don't get the credit for that. That wasn't a *strategic* position, that was a *lucky* position. It easily could have been different, and engaging with the Occupy stuff could have been a much harder decision. It could have had serious consequences for you. Agree?"

"Sure," he says. "I was lucky."

"And Occupy was one of the most interesting things we've ever done. It was complicated and messy and I still don't know how to explain it to people who weren't there. I haven't the slightest clue if we actually did any good or not, but I am glad I was involved. From my perspective, thirty eight year old me who did go through it, it would be a massive bummer if that whole experience were deleted from my life. And it was *luck* that we were lobbed the opportunity to get involved in it, not *strategy*."

He nods.

I lean forward and jab my finger at his chest. "And for the next opportunity that comes along we might not be so lucky. We might be swamped with work. We might have a boss who doesn't get it, who will jeopardize our career if we go for it. Or the opportunity might demand more of our time and energy than we can fit around a full time job. And we'll have to let that opportunity go.

"As a species, a society, as groups of humans all over the world, we need to be positioning ourselves to adapt to the world that is unfolding around us. We need to be able to adapt our social and political systems. We need to be able to adapt our tech stacks, our agglomerations of skills and knowledge of how we interact with the physical world to provide for our basic needs like food, energy, water, shelter, security, and health. And we need to adapt our overall paradigms to the world we find ourselves in. There is a lot of work to do and by the very nature of it— adaptation to an unfolding and destabilizing world—there is no way to plan ahead, to choose one path through the future. The only way we get through this is if we abandon the logic of stability and embrace fluid adaptation. And the starting point for that is for us as individuals to begin in our own lives. We have to cultivate freedom of action in our own lives, break out of the narrow constraints of our maladaptive cultural norms, and begin iterating different approaches. As individuals we have to scrape out autonomy for ourselves so we can begin doing the real work that needs to be done, which is vast and fractal adaptation at all scales of our societies.

"Now is one of the most important times to be alive and engaged because there's so much impact that can be had, to people alive now and to generations and generations of people in the future, and the *environment* is most definitely going to be goddamn *unfolding*, in wild and totally unpredictable ways, and so not possessing strategic personal freedom of action is irresponsible. It is not okay to be stuck, to be trapped, to be unable to duck the fastballs and to be unable to grab on to the beneficial opportunities that arise.

"It's certainly not excusable for anyone who owns *that* book to have their strategic pants down around their ankles," I say, pointing at the book on strategic thinking on the table

There's a long silence between us.

"You talk like what I do at work is irrelevant," he says. "The whole point of why I'm at this company is to work on stuff that matters. To decarbonize the built environment. To make buildings that aren't terrible like all the toxic energy-sucking junk we built in the 20th century. And the built environment uses like 40% of the energy in this country, so that's a huge area to make an impact in. So—the work matters."

"I'm not saying that decarbonization doesn't matter. I'm saying *you* go off the rails and spin out. Is it possible that the most impactful thing you can do is stay at this company or this industry forever and become a badass engineer of the built environment? In which case it doesn't really matter if you have freedom of action outside of work because all that matters is showing up to work and cranking? Sure, maybe."

The Essence of Good Strategy

"That's only one possible scenario though. The essence of good strategy is not to accurately predict the future and execute a plan for it, but to increase your capacity to respond and thrive under a variety of different conditions, so that you can adapt to whatever happens as it unfolds *in order to bring your gifts to the world*. You can't help anyone if you spend the rest of your life scrambling from one personal disaster to the next. And, heads up from the future, things aren't getting *more* stable.

"A lot of things have to be true for sticking it out with this one company or even this industry to be the best plan for you. The economy has to hold together well enough for a building industry to meaningfully exist. There's got to be no other kind of activity you can engage in that's more impactful. The paradigm of working forty to eighty hours a week at a company has to be the best way of delivering your energy and talents to the world." I grimace at this thought.

"Maybe the most impactful thing you can do is write a bunch of books. Or start an ecovillage. Or go independent, freelance, engineer for hire. Or maybe you need to go be a hermit for a year or four, have a revelation on the mountain, and come back down to the world with some brilliant insight. Maybe the best thing for you to do is live a quiet life and putter around a garden, being zen. Maybe this continent becomes engulfed in full scale civil violence, every building you ever worked on gets shelled to rubble, and your true calling is to be a surprisingly good field commander of the fifth generation irregular forces fighting for freedom against the evil of eco-fascism." I thump the book on military strategy that's been my intellectual bible for a decade and a half. "Who knows. The future's gonna get wild, man, global energy descent is no joke. It's never happened before at this scale. We have no idea what's going to happen, how exactly the environment is going to unfold.

"But right now you do not possess the autonomy to pursue almost any of these other options. Because of how your life is arranged, you are locked into one style of action. Having an approximately full time job, working in a corporate setting, choosing from the standard menu. Right now things look like they're going well, but you are walking into a trap. I walked into a trap. I sidelined myself for years because I kept myself locked into this one standard paradigm."

"How do you possibly decide what to do if we're living in a time when the future is so up in the air?" he says.

"The first step isn't to decide what to do. It's to strategically arrange your life such that you preserve as much optionality as possible, so that you can change and adapt quickly as events unfold. That's the missing piece here, that's what I didn't understand. I spent so much time over the next eight years of my life trying to figure out *specifically* what to do, what *plan* to follow, but I should have been working on increasing my freedom of action, and expanding my sense of what was possible. You, right now, are constrained. You're constrained because you need to earn a decent salary in order to pay the bills. At the moment you can't imagine what to do outside of an approximately full time job. You think you need to be an engineer, and you think you need to be an engineer in the way that society defines it. You have narrow ideas of what it means to work, to be a productive member of society.

"Right now you think the good you're doing is that you're decarbonizing the built environment. That is your 'plan', and your ego needs that plan to be an important one. But maybe that's *not* what you're actually doing. Maybe the value of what you're doing at work designing mechanical systems for buildings is making sure that useful materials like copper and steel and glass are all organized in concentrated areas that are easy for future generations of salvagers to find and use for making things that will be actually useful, like pots or copper bells for goats or something."

He rolls his eyes at me.

"I'm not saying that's what I think will happen, but it's dumb to assume the future is going to be as stable as the second half of the last century. Right now is, historically speaking, *extremely strange*. We've never had anything like this before. The characteristics of modern global civilization are entirely dependent on cheap dense easily transportable forms of energy, and as the economics and logic of civilization's energy sources shift to less cheap, less dense, less transportable, it's anyone's guess how that is all going to shake out. You'll go crazy trying to think about it too hard. That is part of why I didn't make much progress for a decade—I just went around and around in circles about this stuff. The solution isn't to figure it all out, it's *to realize that it's not possible to figure it all out* and that you've got to develop an approach to life that accepts that reality."

He rubs his hand over his face. "All right, fine. How do you do that?"

"How to do that is the overall theme of our whole conversation tonight. It's going to take the whole night to unpack. There's another angle on autonomy we need to talk about now. We need to talk about stoke."

Further Reading

Osinga, Frans P.B. (2006). *Science, Strategy, and War: The Strategic Theory of John Boyd,* Routledge.

N.J. Hagens, *Economics for the Future: Beyond the Superorganism.* Ecological Economics Volume 169 (2020), https://doi.org/10.1016/j.ecolecon.2019.106520

Murphy, Tom. (2022, December 19) "The Simple Story of Civilization," *Do the Math.* https://dothemath.ucsd.edu/2022/12/the-simple-story/

Hagens, Nate. *The Great Simplification,* https://www.thegreatsimplification.com/

Hagens, Nate. (Host). (2022, October 26). Daniel Schmachtenberger: "Bend not break #4: Modeling the Drivers of the Metacrisis" [Audio podcast episode]. In *The Great Simplification.* https://www.thegreatsimplification.com/episode/42-daniel-schmachtenberger

4. Stoke Is A Strategic Imperative

"Don't ask what the world needs. Ask what makes you come alive, and go do it. Because what the world needs is people who have come alive."
--Howard Thurman

"Stoke? As in—" he holds his hand up with pinkie and thumb out, and waggles it, "—surf's up, brah?"

"Yes," I say. "The technical term is intrinsic motivation, actions that are their own reward. It's an internal drive towards novel, challenging activity that feels like play and activates all sorts of things like curiosity, knowledge acquisition, and skill development. Stoke drives people to explore, create, learn, seek novel experiences, challenge themselves, and expand their abilities. What might stoke have to do with autonomy?"

"Uh. Stoke. You... need freedom of action to pursue stoke?"

"Sure, yes. That's one thing. More precisely you have to feel autonomous in your decision to pursue stoke. The science is pretty clear that the easiest way to kill it is to try to force it. In fact, you can kill stoke by introducing external rewards for doing it."

"Really?"

"Yeah. They've done studies. Take some kids who draw purely

because they enjoy it. Then start giving them a reward like a candy or a gold sticker when they draw. They might draw a little more. But then take away the reward, and they stop drawing nearly as much as they did before they were given the reward. The external reward killed their stoke. So one of the prerequisites for stoke is autonomy."

"That explains the modern office experience pretty well, then," he mutters.

"What else? Why is stoke important for someone who is concerned about a destabilizing world system?"

He frowns, thinking. "Well, I can see how if someone is left alone to pursue their stoke, they're going to explore their curiosity. They'll follow the activity wherever it leads them. If you do that long enough, you're going to generate a lot of different ways of doing things."

"Yes. And generating a lot of ways of doing things and testing them against reality, that sounds a lot like…"

"Like evolution. Like adaptation," he says.

"Yes. I believe stoke is the engine of adaptation. It's the spontaneous self-directed drive to come up with a bunch of different ways of doing things. As these different ways of doing things come in contact with unfolding environment, successful ones live and unsuccessful ones dies out. The best environmental fits persist and get iterated. There is speculation that this is part of why humans have a dopamine system: stoke is an advantage for a species whose evolutionary strategy is to rapidly adapt to unfolding environmental circumstances by developing new technologies and cultural practices. Evolutionary success depends on a bunch of humans wandering around spontaneously inventing new ways of doing things. And the better they are at generating these new ways, the more successful they'll be at surviving."

He blows out his breath. "That's wild."

"This is my favorite part," I say. "If stoke confers adaptive advantages, and if the essence of strategy is to increase and preserve adaptability, then that means…" I trail off, hoping he'll pick up the thread.

He blinks a few times, thinking, and then his eyes widen. "That means that chasing stoke is a strategic imperative."

"Stoke is a strategic imperative, yes," I say. "Broadly speaking, we ought to chase stoke for the adaptation advantages and not just because it feels good. But it *does* feel good: chasing stoke is a supremely human thing to do, we are literally designed to enjoy the hell out of it. This is really good news. The right thing to do is also deeply satisfying. There are a couple things you need to understand about stoke. The first thing you already figured out: you need autonomy to be able to pursue stoke."

He shrugs. "I mean, sure, that's obvious though. You can't pursue stoke if you're loaded up with obligations."

"Yes, but that's not all. As a state of being, stoke is particular. Conditions have to be just right. It turns out that you can't, for example, order someone to be stoked to do something. The state of stoke requires a sense of agency. You have to believe that you are acting of your own volition, your own desire. If you feel like you're doing something because someone else told you to, if you feel like you don't have much choice in the matter, that's a sure stoke-killer."

"Hm," he says. "That explains why external rewards kill stoke. The external reward must function as a signal that you aren't doing the thing purely because you want to, you're doing it in order to get the gold sticker or whatever."

I nod. "Yes. It casts some doubt on the strategy of seeking to align life's work with salaried employment, doesn't it?"

His eyebrows go up. "Oh."

"Modern work is organized as an almost perfect stoke-killing machine," I say. "I think it has to be risky to mix external rewards like a salary, promotion, and corporate status with important adaptation work, because the constant threat to stoke is so high. Stoke is only an effective adaptation engine because it drives you to explore and try new things— to roam widely, so to speak. Insofar as stoke becomes choked down into narrow approved avenues of activity it ceases to be of much strategic value."

"But when I think of stoke I think of it as a primarily depth focused activity," he says. "When I get stoked on something I just get lost in it and I go super deep," he says.

"Yes. I think it's both. I think that you have to be free to explore widely, and your explorations allow you to discover and then dive deep on activities that you become intrinsically motivated to do. But still, once you start going deep on something, it's essential that you retain the freedom to explore at will within that field of activity and even to go outside of it to connect adjacent activities to it. Novel activity probably plays a big part in the adaptation effect. But you hit on my next point, by bringing up depth. When we're stoked on something we tend to go deep, because it's so enjoyable. The psychological state of pursuing stoke is its own reward because of our dopamine system, we're wired to like it. And what is the result of that?"

"We get really good at it," he says.

"Yes. Take two people who are doing the same kind of activity. The first person is doing it for the money, the trophy, the status, the payoff, or the IPO. The second person is doing it because they're in love with it. Leave them alone for a year or two and who will be better at the end?"

"The second person," he says. "The person who is devoted to it."

I nod. "No matter how much of a disciplined hardass you are, you cannot compete with someone who is in love. Stoke kicks willpower's ass every time."

"But why is this important?" he asks.

"Because things matter now," I say. "The stakes are high. As a species we need to be adapting at all scales, we need to be doing it rapidly so as to cope with the accelerating rate of change of environment, and we need to be as good as we possibly can at it. The quality of our adaptations has to be very, very high, as high as possible, in order to create the most beneficial conditions for humans and all life on the planet."

"But," he says, looking frustrated, "how do we know what to work on, what to be stoked on? How can we know what types of activities will be relevant to the future and which won't?"

I shake my head. "We can't know. And stoke is something that withers with too much imposed direction, so even if we did know it

30

might not do much good. That is one of the defining features of our predicament—it's a crisis of not knowing what to do about the unfolding crises we're in. It's a crisis of knowing we're in a trap but not how to get out of it. One of the reasons we're in the mess we're in is because we adopted a very linear way of thinking about and organizing human activity. We set up a narrow set of guidelines, goals, and values for all of human activity, and we arranged society so most people have little choice but to work on those narrow goals, disconnecting people from access to durable intrinsic motivation.

"Point is, global society constrains the set of acceptable activities humans can engage in to a narrow range, and this narrow range is extremely problematic. Could we come up with a list of new approved activities that will help us get out of the mess we're in? Sure, but the danger is that's the same kind of thinking that got us into this mess in the first place. It risks eco-fascism, unintended consequences, and supposes that humans can analyze and calculate what the earth-system 'needs' us to be doing." I shrug. "Seems dicey to me. I think a better way is to get loads of people to achieve high levels of personal freedom of action and then have them pursue their stoke."

Free 'Em All, Let Gaia Sort 'Em Out

He frowns. "Won't most people just do irrelevant stuff, like make train sets or play video games or make internet memes or whatever?"

"Oh, sure," I say, "definitely. At least as long as the environment they find themselves in is relatively benign. When their environment starts getting weird, though, they'll have the autonomy they need to start adapting in real-time, because they won't be constrained by whatever bullshit options society gives them, like work a full time job or play video games. And until then, even if what they're stoked to do has nothing at all to do with 'solving' the 'Problem' or 'saving the planet' or whatever, it's likely that they'll at least be contributing less to the predicament than if they were still locked in to normal activities."

"What? Why?" he asks.

"Free people doing stuff they love don't need much to be happy. So much of the waste of modern society has to do with the coping mechanisms for living meaningless, unfulfilling lives. We're programmed to buy stuff and experiences to try to fill the void in our hearts, the yearning to go deep on things we love to do and to be connected to other beings. We buy big houses, fast cars, flights to the other side of the world for a long weekend, and cheap entertainment as a way of coping with the unsatisfying, meaningless role we all play in modern society. When we free ourselves and explore our heart's desire, the need to do all that stuff drops away. We don't even need a philosophy of conservation or eco-guilt or anything else. We just need to get free and find what makes us come alive.

"Plus," I add, "The fastest and easiest way to achieve freedom is to learn how to live well on less money. The less money you need to live your ideal lifestyle, the less time you need to spend getting it. People are trapped because they're programmed to always think they need more, so they're never able to carve out any freedom for themselves. When people figure this out, that the claim of advertising that we can buy happiness and a better life is nothing more than an odious lie, their contributions to the project of converting resources into waste heat and pollution will decrease."

"You really think this is the answer?" he says. "Get people to chase stoke and we'll magically save the world?"

"No, man. There is no saving the world. Remember that what we are in right now is not a problem, it is a *predicament*. Problems have solutions. Predicaments have *responses*. At least one viable response to the predicament we're in is to free ourselves rapidly via post-consumer praxis and pursue our stoke. A side effect of people doing this is the emergence of groups of humans who create tech stacks and cultural practices that are more well adapted to the unfolding environment than the current arrangement. I have some guesses as to what those groups will look like, but I could be wrong. So I want people to be as free as possible to pursue their stoke and let real interaction with environment point towards the best adaptations."

"Free them all and let Gaia sort them out, huh?" he says.

I tilt my head at him. "Yes, actually. That's a great way of putting it."

"Okay, so, let me try to get this straight," he says. "Stoke, aka intrinsic motivation, is part of the human ability to rapidly adapt to unfolding environment, which is largely responsible for our evolutionary success. Broadly speaking, tying this in to Boydian theory, the ability to act under conditions of stoke confers strategic adaptive advantages. Not only does stoke lead to exploration of the option landscape, thereby developing a broad set of possible responses to unfolding environmental conditions, people tend to be better and get better at stuff that they're stoked to do because the neurochemistry of stoke sets up intrinsic reward feedback loops that people can ride to mastery. But since a prerequisite of stoke is autonomy, it is difficult or impossible to direct or externally reward stoke via salaries, status, or whatever. So the more people who somehow attain high levels of autonomy, the better, because that'll increase the population of people capable of chasing stoke. Which, as unfolding environment places further pressure on society to adapt, it seems likely that many of our best responses to predicament will come from this process."

"That's the idea, at the group level, yes," I say. "It also works at the individual level. If you free yourself and are able to chase your stoke, you're going to develop broader and deeper competencies, improving your ability to respond to whatever the future brings."

"I still feel like you're implying that totally random stoke pursuit is going to magically result in responses to real predicaments. I just don't see that," he says.

"Stoke pursuit is never random. What people choose to pursue inevitably comes from their worldview, their perspective on the world, their ethics and values, and the information they get from their environment. Even if those ethics and values are unconscious or emergent. If someone is a militant vegan they're in little danger of their stoke leading them to become a really good butcher. Similarly, you are in little danger of inventing a better way to hydrofrack tar sands, or to build a better diesel supercharger. Your agency would not lead you there."

"So you're saying we need to improve people's values or ethics," he says.

"Not at all. Other people are outside of my realm of control. I'm not giving policy advice, I'm giving *you* advice. And I know what your values and ethics are, deep down, and I obviously agree with them, and so we don't need to talk about them. If you can get free, if you can put yourself in a position to have the time and space to pursue your stoke, your values will guide you to competence and adaptation in activities in alignment with them. Since you're so obsessed with the various issues of the metacrisis, and since you spend your free time loading your brain with strategic theory, I'm not too worried that you're going to drop yourself into a hole playing video games or inventing a better nerf gun."

"Oh," he says. "Right. Okay."

"The trap I was in over the next eight years of my life wasn't a philosophy trap, it wasn't a trap of not knowing what I thought was meaningful in the world," I say. "I had a good idea of what I wanted to be doing and working on, but I couldn't figure out how to get there from where I was. I was stuck banging my head on a brick wall, spinning like a tire in sand. What I'm explaining is how to get unstuck, to get moving again. To attain freedom of action.

"This explains why I'm not here to tell you *what* the best thing to focus on is. I trust you to figure that out on your own with stoke as your guide. The whole point is not to rely on luck or brilliance to choose the right thing to focus on, but to arrange your affairs such that you can adapt and provide value no matter what happens. Maybe your life looks like another five years of engineering, then two years meditating and taking mushrooms in a hermitage in the desert, then three years being a wandering activist, then you write a book, then you start an activist/ecovillage project that grows into a whole thing and connects up with the Transition Town movement, and then people are coming to you asking how to make their projects like yours, and then by the time you're my age you're helping loads of people get their own lives pointed in the right direction, resilient, ready for the world they actually are going to have to live in."

He frowns. "How could I pull that off? I'm not after the big bucks, you know that, but nobody's gonna pay me anything to sit in a cave in the desert for two years. How do I make money doing that?"

I smile at him. "I'm telling you that when the time comes, you won't have to. This is the first real secret. If you remember nothing else from what I say tonight, remember this: learning to live well at a very low cost of living is *magic*."

Further Reading

Di Domenico SI, Ryan RM. (2017, March 24). *The Emerging Neuroscience of Intrinsic Motivation: A New Frontier in Self-Determination Research*. Front Hum Neurosci. 2017;11:145.

Pink, Daniel H. (2009). *Drive: The Surprising Truth About What Motivates Us*. Riverhead Books.

Wheal, Jamie (2021). *Recapture the Rapture: Rethinking God, Sex, and Death in a World That's Lost Its Mind*. Harper.

Csikszentmihalyi, Mihaly. (2008). *Flow: The Psychology of Optimal Experience*. Harper Perennial Modern Classics.

Kotler, Steven. (2014). *The Rise of Superman: Decoding the Science of Ultimate Human Performance*. New Harvest.

Kotler, Steven. (2021). *The Art of Impossible: A Peak Performance Primer*. Harper.

"Self Determination Theory," accessed August 28, 2023, https://selfdeterminationtheory.org/theory/

5. Frugality is for Losers

They realize, many of them, that the lifestyles that industrial societies provide even to their more privileged inmates are barren of meaning and value, that the pursuit and consumption of an endless series of increasingly shoddy manufactured products is a very poor substitute for a life well lived, and that stepping outside the narrowing walls of a world defined by the perks of the consumer economy is the first step toward a more meaningful existence.
--John Michael Greer

He holds my gaze. I wait.

"You traveled back in time to a different dimension on a rainy-ass night to tell me to cut back on my spending habits a bit?" he says. "To be frugal?"

"No, not to be frugal," I shake my head. "Frugality is meaningful only in the context of consumerism. I'm not here to tell you to become a frugal consumer or to make a budget. I'm telling you to internalize post-consumer praxis. Frugal consumerism sucks. Post-consumerism is awesome.

"Right now you're only a little in debt. But starting next year you spend every dollar that goes into your checking account, and then even more. You start accumulating consumer debt. You think you're part of the solution because you design energy efficient buildings and join street protests but you're just as programmed by the construct of consumer ideology as anyone else. You talk good theory about how we need a different paradigm, an ecological civilization, but you don't see your own total obedience to the system you yourself claim is wrecking the planet and infantilizing the population."

He gives me a hard look. "I *do* believe in an ecological civilization. But it doesn't exist yet. I can't somehow live outside of something I can't escape."

"No. That is wrong," I say. "The womb of any future society is your mind. And your heart. The seeds of an ecological society, if they exist, are carried in the minds and hearts of humans for whom that vision is so real they can taste it. The work of midwifing the world you want is to act as if it is real already, to create it in the nooks and crannies of the existing world. For you, the reality of the world you want can become more real than the mass hallucination that exists for everyone else. Then you go find other people who see it too, and you work with them, and together you build, and bit by bit the vision that doesn't exist yet grows infrastructure, networks, groups, and organizations. The ideas replicate through the incumbent construct and eventually you find that you are living in pockets of the new world, and these pockets are growing and connecting and spreading. As the old world crumbles the new one sprouts out of its ruins. And the seedpod of that new world is between your ears."

"But I do spend a lot of time thinking about an ecological society, a better world," he protests. "When I'm at work I'm helping with the infrastructure and at home I'm reading about permaculture and history and philosophies of ecological governance and—"

"—and yet those ideas will not trickle down to your day to day lifestyle, not deep enough anyway, and you will spend all of your money and you will go into five figure consumer debt," I say evenly. "The seeds of a better world will lie fallow on the soil of your mind for a decade. Fundamentally, structurally, as evidenced by your actions, you will not be fertile soil for the world you want to see born. Right now you see the path as a set of technical infrastructure projects that you want to build. You are skipping steps, trying to jump ahead to the fun stuff. You are trying to change the world without first changing yourself. You can only cause pain if you continue in this way.

"I'm not trying to tear you down, I'm giving you a warning in good faith. You've got malware running up here," I say, tapping my forehead. "It's not your fault. The operating system of our society loads it into everyone's heads without their consent. I'm not telling you you're a bad person. I'm telling you that if you really do want to be part of building a better world, you've got to go even deeper into yourself than you already have. And even when you clear out all the dysfunctional programming you'll have to stay vigilant so you don't get reinfected. Every morning you have to choose to take the red pill again."

He rubs his face in his hands. "So what's the number? How little do I need to spend?"

I shake my head. "There is no number."

He looks frustrated. "You *just said* that below a certain threshold—"

"And that threshold depends on the person, the circumstance, their goals, vision for their life, risk tolerance, the macroeconomic condition. It changes year by year. If I give you a specific number you'll focus on that and at best make quantitative changes to your life. You can spend almost nothing and still keep all the consumer malware loaded in your head, still be just as embedded in the construct as anyone else. For some people that's fine but for you and me it's not enough. We want to qualitatively, fundamentally decouple our brains from…" I gesture vaguely around us, "…from the infantilization of mainstream consumer society.

"If all you do is force yourself to spend very little money without changing yourself *up here*," I tap my temple again, "your life will suck. It will be sacrifice and pointless hardship. You'll be playing poverty tourism. That is not what I'm talking about and you need to understand that."

"I need something to hold on to," he says. "This is too abstract. How much money do you spend? Give me a ballpark number."

I glare at him for a moment, then say "Fine. For the past three years I've averaged about ten thousand dollars a year. I've been as low as seven thousand and as high as fourteen but the running average is about ten. I'm pretty sure that'll drop down to between five and seven thousand a year once I finish a couple of projects."

"Jesus," he says. "Do you just eat bread and water and shoplift clothes or something?"

"No. I live an abundant and adventurous life. My *expenses* are well below the federal poverty level, but I live richly. There is a difference. I figured out how to reject consumer ideology in my own life while still living within a consumer society, by internalizing post-consumer praxis."

Consumer Ideology and Post-Consumer Praxis

He shakes his head. "You've said this a couple times now, post-consumer praxis. What do you mean by that?"

"That's Jacob's term," I say. "A lot of people recognize there's a problem with how our society functions, and they insist that corporations should supply them with greener or more sustainable options. They don't accept personal responsibility for their actions because they can't even see outside the paradigm of consumerism. Which, in their defense, is difficult. The paradigm of consumption is the water we swim in. We're not taught to see consumerism as a choice, we're taught that it's just how the world works. We're not given any stories about lifestyles that function any different, so for the most part the only thing we can imagine is a greener, more eco version of the consumer paradigm. Some people get how this isn't good enough, but don't know what to do about it. So they're stuck feeling guilt and shame for living the only way they've been shown how.

"Post-consumer praxis is that alternative pragmatic approach to building a life. It says, 'right, *hell* with this, I'm not going to participate in consumerism, but I'm not going to stop there. I'm going to actively participate in a new and different way of relating to the world and society. Right now, today. I'm not going to demand it of anyone else, I'm not going to beg politicians to save me from clearance sales and strip malls, I'm going to make it a reality in my own life, right now, right here, and not make a big fuss about it.'"

"You really think consumerism is the source of all our problems?" He says. "And if we solve that we solve everything?"

I shake my head. "Again, we don't have problems, we have a predicament. Right now the infection of consumerism has our species set on a path of eating the world. It is clear that one of the things we've got to do is root consumerism out of our cultural programming, and until we do so it will eat all of our solutions, our energy efficiency measures, our clever green innovations, and turn them into greenwashed illusions. Look, what is consumerism?"

"What?"

"What actually is consumerism?" I say. "The -ism indicates an ideology, right? What are we talking about?"

"Consumerism is where the purpose of life is to consume stuff, to convert resources into waste and call the process GDP," he says.

"Yes," I say. "It's the idea – often implicit – that increasing consumption is a good thing and should be a primary goal, for individuals and for society."

"Right," he continues. "The concept of citizenship used to be that people had a fair amount of independence and autonomy, and the purpose of governance was to stay out of the way as much as possible and make sure no one got too screwed over by power imbalances. But how to live a good life was supposed to be largely self determined – the whole point was to create an environment, a society, where humans can flourish on their own terms. I mean, that was the idea, I don't know if that was ever a reality."

"And now what's the deal?" I ask.

"Citizens have been infantilized into consumers who are in service to the economy. The government is in service to the economy. The economy has become the thing that is being optimized for now, and human flourishing has taken a backseat."

"Yes. There is no evil cabal of people who intentionally enslave people to serve the economy. This situation came about because people noticed that when the economy is growing, people get pulled up out of poverty, fewer people die of cholera, the state can spend more money on infrastructure for things like sanitation and libraries and roads and all the rest. It came from humanistic origins. It just got out of hand. And now we as consumers exist for the good of the economy, the Machine, the Superorganism, the construct."

"Okay, I understand that," he says.

"Most people understand that at the mass scale of society, but at the level of the individual, what is consumerism? What is the basic problem solving approach of consumerism?"

"Consumerism is the ideology that buying stuff is the only way to solve your problems," he says.

"Bingo. That's it. Consumer ideology says you solve problems by spending money. Money is a hammer, and there are no other tools, so all problems are nails. If you're bored, you buy a Netflix subscription. If you're tired, you buy a coffee. If you're stressed, you buy a massage chair. If your toilet breaks, you call a plumber. If you feel like a loser, you buy a nicer car or a new outfit. If you feel unfit, you buy a membership at a gym, or a rower, or one of those electrical ab shocker things.

"It goes further than that. It permeates our thinking as a society. We're incapable of thinking beyond the consumerism box. If fossil fuels are polluting the atmosphere the solution is to buy an electric car. Microplastics are filling up the oceans; buy really expensive all natural fabric clothing and throw your old stuff out. Global temperatures are rising; buy an enormous space mirror. That's the ideology of consumerism. And money is useful as a medium of exchange for goods and services, but there are other ways of solving problems. It's like we're in a workshop full of tools but we use only one.

"It's not that the tool we're using is evil, it's that insisting on only using one tool is stupid and the effects *look* evil, like how using a claw hammer instead of a saw to cut a board looks like something an insane clown would do as performance art. We've gone as far as we can go with this one problem-solving tool, buying stuff, and it's time for us as a society to add some other problem solving methods to our tool kit.

"But that's society. It starts at the personal level, the household level. This is what I'm talking about. Learning a post-consumer lifestyle means learning other ways of solving problems than just buying stuff. It isn't rocket science."

"Okay," he says. "What are the other methods of solving problems besides money?"

"Being competent, broadly speaking. In-sourcing competence rather than outsourcing, at the household level. Developing a wide range of skills. Internalizing a producer mindset rather than a consumer mindset. Developing a rich social world, being part of a community. Also becoming a better strategic thinker, learning to think in systems rather than in linear disconnected silos. It is very important to understand that post-consumerism is not merely being frugal or cheap. Learning how to get stuff without paying much for it is clever and highly optimized consumerism, but it's still consumerism. Finding killer sales and clipping coupons is not post-consumerism.

"But internalizing post-consumerism takes a while. It's not an overnight thing. I'm five years in and still think of myself as a beginner. If you just say 'right, great, skills and systems thinking, I'll get on it', while still being inside a full time really stressful job, while still being inside a web of consumer obligations, while still not being free because if you lose your job you'll be out on your ass in a month, you're going to crash and burn. Or just skim off the surface without really being able to change your life at a deeper level."

He shakes his head. "I don't see how I can be effective if I'm spending all of my time scraping by below the poverty line."

I shake my head. "No. See, this is what I mean. You've got modern consumer ideology so loaded up in your brain you can't imagine what I'm talking about. You assume that options, power, and quality of life are linearly proportional to the amount of money you spend. You assume that a low cost of living implies hardship and scarcity. But that's wrong."

First World Problems

"Listen, in 2019 before I got into this stuff I spent all of my take home income, which was about seventy thousand dollars. I drank good beer, good coffee, and good whiskey. I ate good food, both from restaurants and from grocery stores. I bought a motorcycle just for fun. If I needed some gear for a trip, I bought it. If my truck broke, I paid to get it fixed. I drove a lot of miles. I wanted to travel, but my girlfriend didn't have a remote job, so I asked to her to quit and come with me and I paid for her expenses too. If we got tired of living in my cargo trailer conversion, I rented a furnished apartment for us for a couple months. Life was easy in that respect. I solved all my problems with money.

"On the flip side, I worked full time and was not free to do whatever I wanted. I was stressed. I had existential issues with the meaning and purpose of my career. A lot of the beer and whiskey I drank was to take the edge off of the stress and my uncertainty about how I was showing up in the world. I very much felt like I was struggling to get to a point where I could start living my real life, but I wasn't actually making any progress. I didn't have time or energy to spend on activities that I felt were really meaningful to me. I didn't have enough time to devote to myself, to my girlfriend, and my job, not to mention everyone else in my life who I cared about.

"I also knew that even though I bought organic, fair trade, green certified products that my footprint was more than the earth could support if everyone lived like I did. I knew I was taking more than my fair share, and that bothered me. My life was abundant in the narrow terms of consumer goods I could buy, but I wasn't living a *good* life by my own values, by my own inner scorecard. I was just scraping by."

"You had a nice life and you were angsty about it. How very first world problems of you," he says.

"Yeah, I *was* angsty about my nice first-world life," I say. "Because I understood what the consequences of my nice life were for other people. Because I knew that I, and everyone else, were participating in a dysfunctional system that was ripping the planet apart and infantilizing

43

the human race. Because by that point I could no longer drink my fancy beers and eat my nice food and sleep in nice beds in safe neighborhoods without feeling the pain of species going extinct, without tasting the ashes of the wildfires in my dreams, without wondering what it feels like to die in a heat wave, without feeling like I and everyone else were living in one big trap. None of those consequences were my fault, but I couldn't un-know them. And I couldn't go on like that. I couldn't just forget about it."

I take a few breaths to calm down. "Okay. That was 2019, yeah? I spent most of my money, went on trips, and had nice things. It was the same the year before that, and the year before that, and the year before that. I lived in Europe for four months in 2016. Greece, Spain, France, London. Two months in Greece in 2017. In 2018 I lived the vanlife in the mountains. On paper, or rather, on Instagram, if I'd bothered to post about it, it looked fantastic."

Living an Abundant Life Spending Almost Nothing

"But now you don't spend any money and have a really isolated, boring, and irrelevant life," he says.

I roll my eyes. "In 2022 I lived in Europe for *six* months. Portugal, Morocco, France, Scotland. I lived in a treehouse with a French guy and a cat, built a solar thermal panel with an open source CNC machine, rebuilt an aquaponics system on a permaculture community on the Isle of Skye, made mud bricks within sight of the Algerian border in the Dra'a River Valley of Morocco, fell asleep on a park bench in Lille with a copy of Camus on my chest with croissant crumbs in my beard, learned how to listen to the birds from an autistic anti-war activist, and had a dance party with a bunch of European dirtbags on the top of a hill at sunset among wind turbines overlooking the South Coast of Portugal on an offgrid maker farm."

I lean forward and say, "And I spent ten thousand dollars total that year. Not isolated, not boring, and not irrelevant." I lean back and continue.

"In twenty twenty three I rode my bike a thousand miles to a wedding and a music festival, organized a weekend retreat for pioneers of cooperative self-sufficiency practices, and spent a month and a half in Japan building offgrid infrastructure. I also spent ten thousand dollars that year. So. Tell me again how low spending equals an isolated and boring life."

I shake my head. "To me it feels like when I had the full time job and bought whatever I liked, *that* was scraping by. Spiritually. Existentially. I was always just half a step ahead of being consumed by despair. I wasn't free to do the work I knew needed to be done and that I knew I was meant for. My life was physically comfortable, but I could barely stand it. Now I'm the most engaged with what I'm doing I've ever been. I feel like I'm living my life. I'm not waiting for my life to begin, I'm not hustling now for some vague payoff in the future. I am, every single day, full of the sensation that I am living my own life."

He looks frustrated. "Okay, but again, how do you actually pull it off? Like you keep saying, I'm not free to not work. I've got to make money one way or another. How do I get from here to there, to this post-consumer praxis, to living on very little?"

"Living *well* on very little," I correct him. "It's not enough to just play poverty tourism. The point is to learn the ways in which you can live a good, abundant, rich life without using much money to get it. The point is to develop your other problem-solving methods. Consumerism isn't the practice of spending a *lot* of money, it's the practice of *only* spending money to solve your problems. This is what must be unlearned."

He looks ready to blow up on me so I hold up my hands. "Yes, let's talk about how to actually pull it off now."

Further Reading

Peter Limberg, interview with Jacob Lund Fisker, "A Systems Approach to Resilient Lifestyle Design w/Jacob Lund Fisker," YouTube video, *The Stoa*, February 9, 2021, https://youtu.be/SPvftqB-WXk?si=8JxNGOLUQVqxtb_k

Peter Limberg, interview with Jacob Lund Fisker, "Resolving the Meta-Crisis with Emergent Movement and Post-Consumerist Praxis w/ Jacob Lund Fisker," YouTube video, *The Stoa,*, September 2, 2021, https://youtu.be/0MGQgQZHx1Q?si=eCgTgJrGQw3-4LaZ

Zehner, Ozzie. (2012). *Green Illusions: The Dirt Secrets of Clean Energy and the Future of Environmentalism.* University of Nebraska Press.

Alexander, Samuel. (2017). *Art Against Empire: Towards an Aesthetics of Degrowth.*

6. The Crowbar Of Freedom

"First, drop your cost of living as far below your income as you can. While you're saving money you develop your practical skills as much as you can. You use your skills and surplus of money to acquire more freedom, which gives you even more time to develop skills."

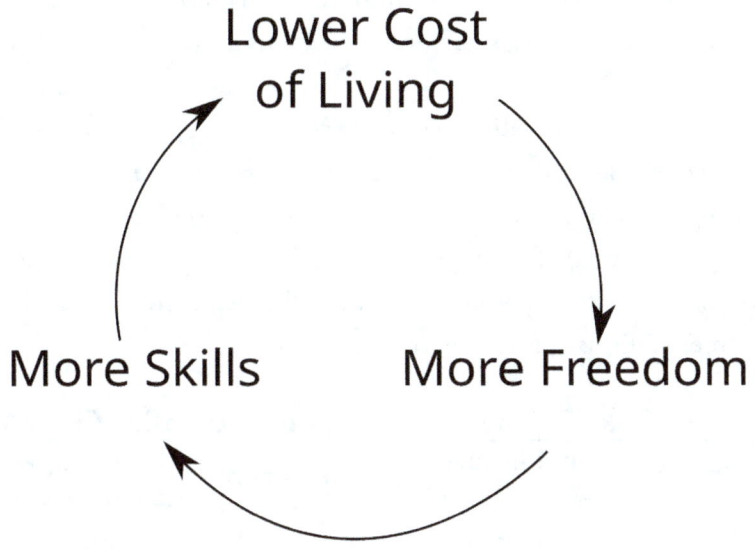

"This works like a ratchet. The more skills you have, the less money you need. The less money you need, the easier it is to attain freedom.

The more freedom you get, the more time you can spend developing skills. Crank this skill ratchet until you're as free as you want to be and then do whatever you want. It's a positive feedback loop. Make sense?"

He shrugs. "Simple enough in theory. But how do you spend less than ten thousand dollars a year and not have a crappy life? I just don't see it."

"Let's talk it through. What's your salary right now?"

"Sixty five thousand," he says.

"Okay. So after taxes and stuff, let's call it fifty you get to take home. I'll just round everything off to keep it simple. About how much do you spend a year?"

"Thirty five thousand," he says.

"So you save fifteen thousand a year," I say. "How many years is that?"

"What do you mean how many years is that?" he asks.

"How many years of freedom do you save a year? If you save fifteen thousand dollars a year, and you spend thirty five thousand dollars a year, how much time does fifteen thousand dollars buy you?"

"Oh. That's just savings divided by expenses, which is… about five months."

"You earn less than half a year of freedom every year you work. It'd take you more than a decade to earn five years of freedom. That's not good enough. What if you only spend ten thousand a year?"

"That's four years of savings every year. In five years I'd have twenty years of savings, in ten years I'd have… I'd have forty." He blinks a couple times as he says this. His frown softens.

Income $50k, CoL $35k

$$\text{Freedom} = \frac{\text{Annual Savings}}{\text{Cost of Living}}$$

$$= \frac{\$15{,}000}{\$35{,}000}$$

Freedom = 0.43 years

Income $50k, CoL $10k

$$\text{Freedom} = \frac{\text{Annual Savings}}{\text{Cost of Living}}$$

$$= \frac{\$40{,}000}{\$10{,}000}$$

Freedom = 4 years

"And what if," I say, "just imagine for a second, what if you do what you now think is impossible and learn to live off of five thousand dollars a year?"

He shakes his head in disbelief but says, "I'd earn nine years of freedom every year. In five years I'd have forty-five years of freedom. In ten years I'd have ninety years of freedom."

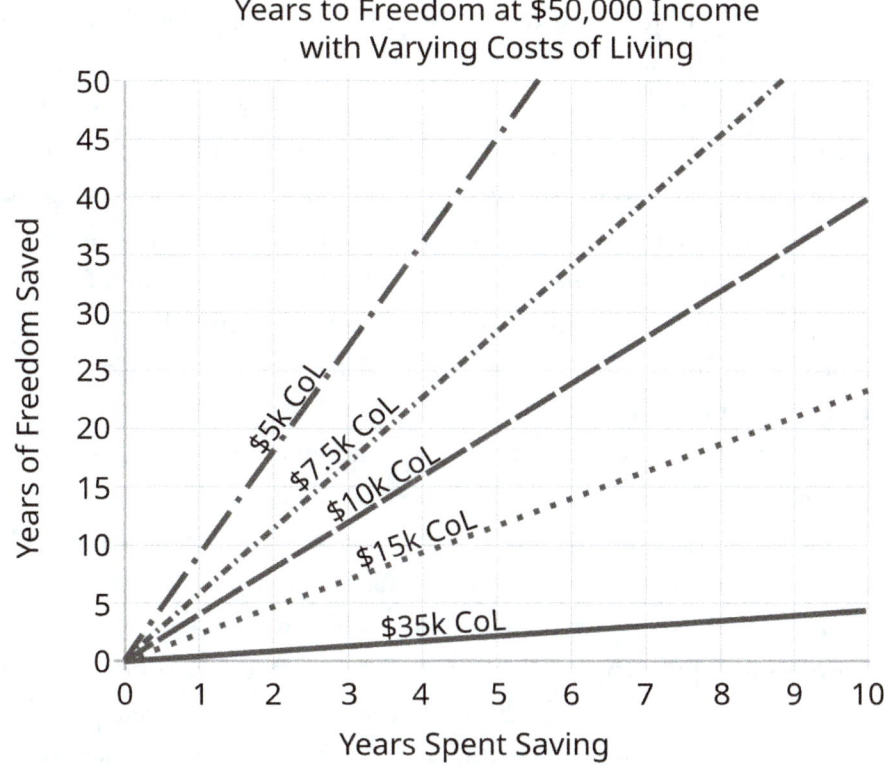

Years to Freedom at $50,000 Income with Varying Costs of Living

"Math is fun, huh?"

Free in Five Years

He shakes his head. "But how do you spend so little and not have a shit life? I don't understand."

"That's because you're thinking like a frugal consumer, which sucks," I say. "Your strategy is consumerism and you are reaching the end of what streamlined consumerist tactics can do for you. You need better strategy, a different mindset. The answer isn't to try *harder*, it's to try *different.* If you do the work to change your perspective, the day to day tactical decisions actually get easier. There *isn't* a way to cut your expenses by a third or more *as a consumer.* No way to clip enough coupons, find enough deals, scrounge enough thrift shops to build a cheap consumer-based life on that little money, I agree. Not an attractive life, anyway. In order to get your expenses this low, you have to cheat."

"What, you mean like tax fraud?" he asks.

I shake my head. "You don't need to do anything illegal to live this way. In fact I highly recommend against looking for illegal shortcuts — it's not necessary and the risk of penalties makes it a dumb strategy. Keep your nose clean. No, what I mean is that you have to realize that you're playing a different game. Everyone else is playing the consumerism game, the whoever-dies-with-the-most-toys-wins game. We're choosing not to play that game. In order to pull this off, you've got to learn new skills and you've got to apply systems thinking to how you run your life. You've got to spin up a permaculture design for your lifestyle, essentially."

"A permaculture design? You mean the only way to do it is to grow your own food?"

"I'm all for growing your own food, but that's not what I mean. One of the fundamental insights of permaculture design is that if you arrange the components of a system such that the outputs from one become the inputs for another, so that all of the components of the system function harmoniously, then the resource requirements from outside of the system are very low, and the diversity and richness of the system itself goes up. The ideal permaculture system runs on solar income and rainwater, and otherwise meets all of the system's needs from within the system itself. That style of thinking is what you've got to apply to your own life, if you want to free yourself rapidly. If you want to become a post-consumer and engage in the process of being useful to the world you want."

"That sounds maddeningly complex. I don't see how it's possible," he says.

"You don't have to. You just have to begin. Look, spend as much money as you want. But know what it is you're spending: your time. Your autonomy. Your life energy. The purpose of showing you how much freedom you could theoretically earn if you only spent five or ten thousand a year isn't to convince you that that's what you *ought* to spend. It's to make you understand what's possible so you can make your own decision about how to run your life. If you can figure out how to save 85% of your income, you only have to work for about five years to save up enough money to fund the rest of your life, because thirty years of expenses is about enough of a stash to build a perpetual portfolio. There's something magic about a very low cost of living. If you can live off of fifteen percent of your income, you can achieve a remarkable level of freedom-of-action within five years, and you don't need to win the lottery to do it."

He's frowning. Free in five years sounds good, but I know that spending less than ten thousand a year sounds impossible to him.

The Subtle Art of the Crowbar

"Let's walk through how to pull this off. Keep in mind that what we're trying to do isn't to figure out how to spend less money. We're trying to change our mindset to one where we simply don't need to spend very much money to have the life of our dreams. We are trying to change something fundamental about our *identity* – we're trying to change how we think about the world. There is a relationship between our actions and our beliefs, and sometimes you have to take a bit of a leap of faith."

"Man, this is getting woo," he shakes his head. "What do you mean, a leap of faith?"

"It's one thing to speak abstractly about a post-consumer mindset. It's another thing entirely to switch your daily actions to align with a post-consumer identity. Part of the process is to intentionally engage in actions that might not make sense to you as part of the process of changing your identity. The more post-consumer action you take, the more you observe yourself acting as a post-consumer, the more you begin to believe it, and the more automatic the behavior becomes. An example of this is doing a No-Buy Year."

"A year where you don't buy anything?" he says. "At all?"

"Pay for bills, groceries, rent, taxes – only essential expenses, is the idea of the classic No-Buy Year," I say. "The nice thing about it is that it's simple. You don't have to make a lot of decisions every day. All you have to do is not buy stuff. What we're trying to do is break ourselves of the habit of automatically solving our problems with money, right? The quickest way to do that is to actually stop buying stuff. This is an example of the Crowbar Method, which is what I did and I recommend for you."

"What's the alternative?" he asks.

"There's the incremental method where you make small, incremental changes, one at a time. It's designed to never make you too uncomfortable. It takes longer to see results, but it's good for people who don't deal well with drastic change and also people who have families who aren't totally on board."

"And the crowbar method is, what, just do it all at once?" he asks.

I nod. "As much as you can. It still takes some time to internalize but, yes, the crowbar method is to get your cost of living as low as possible as fast as possible and force yourself to stop solving all of your problems with money. This is key. The point of the No Buy Year and the Crowbar Method is not to reduce expenses or to go without. It is to fast-track your skills at solving problems with tools other than money.

"You also happen to start earning lots of freedom right away, whereas with the incremental approach you slowly ramp up to higher savings rates. It's uncomfortable and can freak out the people in your life, but it's very effective."

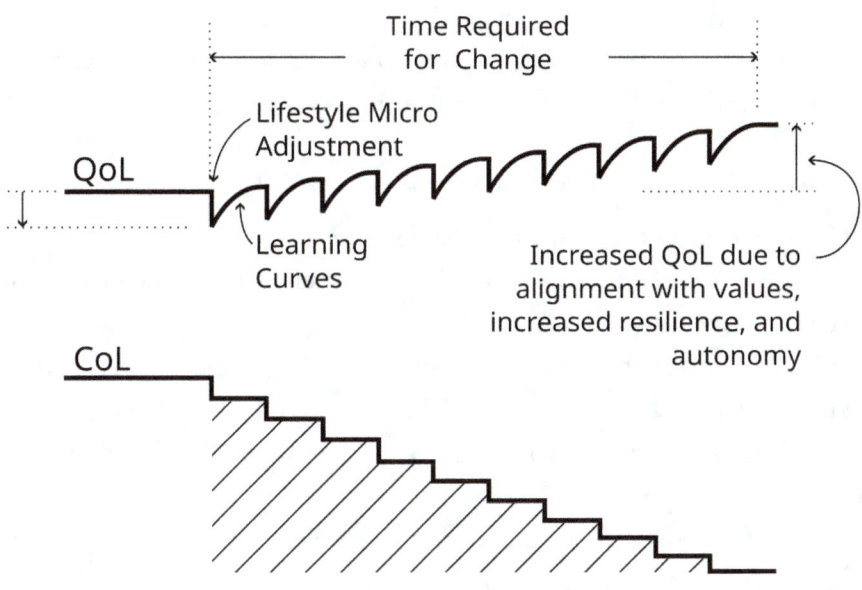

The Incremental Method

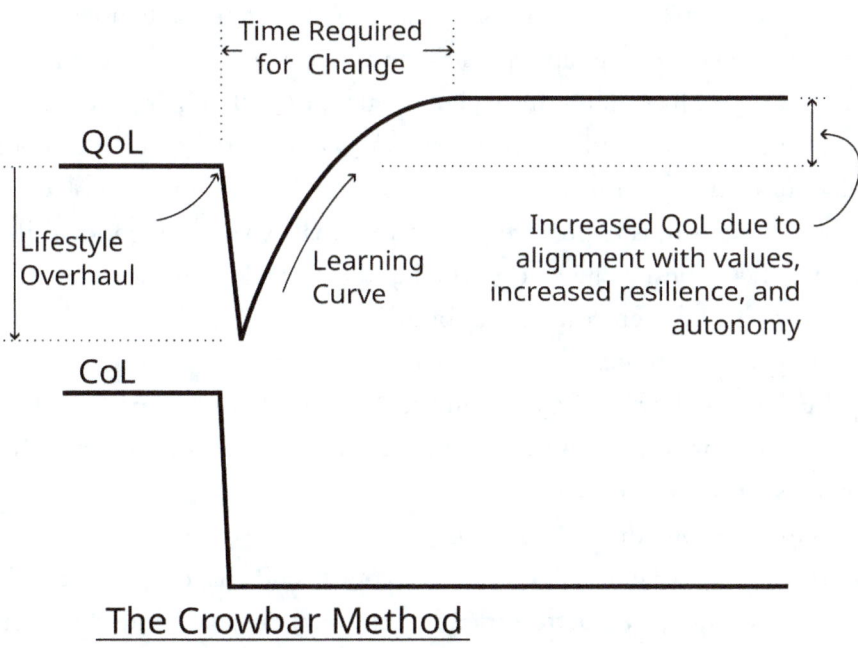

The Crowbar Method

"Okay, so, I just do this crowbar No Buy Year thing, and that's it?"

"Keep the No-Buy Year in mind but let's look at your expenses strategically, first. What are your current biggest expenses?"

Lifestyle Design Strategy

He thinks. "Rent, obviously. And food. Rent is a grand, with utilities it's around twelve hundred. I probably spend eight hundred a month on food, restaurants, and bars."

"Good. Food is the simplest. Stop eating and drinking at restaurants and bars, eat way less or no meat, and learn to cook all of your meals."

He looks at me as if expecting me to continue. I hold his gaze and say nothing.

"But—if I stop going out, that's my whole social life," he protests. "That's where everyone hangs out."

"I didn't say stop *going* to restaurants and bars. I said stop eating and drinking there. Go with your friends, but don't order anything. Get a seltzer and pretend to be DDing, tip the bartender a couple bucks. Better yet, start organizing picnics and bbq's at parks and in your backyard more. Just doing this will cut your food bill in half at least.

"Then, I recommend you stop drinking alcohol altogether. You could limit your drinking, or brew your own, and that's fine. But alcohol, either way you look at it, is expensive poison that makes you less good at life." I shrug. "It's easiest to just stop drinking the stuff. It's only difficult for a week or two, and then you forget about it."

"Do you not drink anymore?" he asks.

"I drink one bottle of good whiskey a year," I say. "Tim always gets me one for Christmas. And I might have a couple beers on my birthday. Otherwise, no, and I don't miss it."

"Man, everyone drinks. I'd be the weirdo."

"You say that like it's a bad thing. If your friends have a problem with you not drinking, get better friends. Anyway, do that, and then start paying attention to how much ingredients cost at the grocery store, and learn to cook tasty food that isn't more expensive than it needs to be,

54

and you can get your food bill below $200 without much effort. That's at lest $7,200 a year you're not blowing on alcohol and food, and you'll be healthier.

"Then, rent. Rent is the hardest, especially here in the Bay. It is legitimately difficult. You're going to have to get creative here. It's possible you could find a cool spot in a warehouse space somewhere for less than five hundred a month, but that'd be a lucky break and the neighborhood would probably be sketchy.

"The most attractive option for you is to pull a Robin Greenfield and find a homeowner who is willing to let you build a tiny house in their backyard in exchange for fixing up the place, planting a garden, helping with chores, whatever. There are plenty of older people around here who'd love to help out a young guy trying to make a difference in the world and do something interesting, and have him around to hang out with every once in a while.

"There are other ways to get around paying normal Bay area rents, but something like that is the best fit for you. The beauty of it is that once you build that tiny house, you've got basic shelter solved. You've unlocked super low shelter costs just about anywhere by virtue of having built that. And once you do the symbiotic relationship with a homeowner once, you've got a reference and a reputation. You could do it anywhere and it gets easier every time as your reputation grows.

"So, do that, and you can get your shelter cost of living down below five hundred, possibly even closer to zero depending on the relationship you cultivate. You'll learn skills building the tiny house, gardening maybe, you'll learn from your relationship with the owner, and you'll become a more well-rounded human. It's full of positive side effects."

"That actually sounds fun," he says. "It'd be difficult to get enough time to build a tiny house with work, but if I can pull it off it'd be fun."

I smile. "I converted a cargo trailer in 2018 and have been living in it ever since. I love it. So that's food and shelter. Most people have high transportation costs but you don't because you don't own a car and ride your bike to work. Make sure wherever you park your tiny house is within biking distance to work and you're good."

"Wait, wouldn't I need a truck to tow the tiny house?" he asks.

"Only when you move it, which is infrequent, so just borrow or rent one when necessary," I say. "Okay, those are the big expenses taken care of. The rest is mostly a mop up operation. What's the next biggest thing you spend money on?"

He thinks. "Trips? Renting a car, a flight, airbnbs, that sort of thing. I don't go on trips often but they're always a few grand each."

I nod. "Trips are expensive when you work full time in one location, because everyone thinks you have to go far away. It's insane. Luckily, you live in California. You have access to good weather somewhere nearby all year round, and beautiful beaches, forests, and mountains accessible within a few hours in any direction. Just don't go far, and don't rent stupid expensive airbnbs and trips don't have to cost any more than your normal life."

"But what about, like, seeing the world, and experiencing other cultures, and stuff like that?" he says. "That seems important. I'm not willing to only ever experience the cultural bubble of the US."

I nod. "Definitely. Do travel, but do it in a couple years, when you're done working, or take a sabbatical, or negotiate working remotely, so you can give that experience all of your attention instead of cramming it into a week or two of vacation time. If you travel slow and strategically, international travel doesn't have to cost more than your normal life. In fact, it can cost less. But flying out of California to take a trip in beautiful mountains somewhere on the other side of the world for a few days, which isn't enough time to come down from the stress of work much less the stress of fast travel, is just a waste of money and resources. Be smart about it."

"That makes sense."

"Everything else is minor details. You don't need to buy so many books because libraries exist. You don't need an expensive cell data plan, wifi is everywhere and you can get pay as you go plans for emergencies for a few bucks a month. With a little effort you can dress sharp for almost nothing with the thrift stores around here. With just a little strategic thinking, and application of your values and what you want in the world, we've just gotten your expenses down below ten thousand a year. I don't remember what else you spend money on, but the No Buy Year will take care of them."

"That actually doesn't sound that hard now that you've walked through it a bit," he says.

"It is honestly embarrassing how straightforward it is to spend very little if you just, like, try," I say. "Especially because you're single with no dependents. It gets a lot trickier if you try to do this with a family. Not impossible, the same principles work, it's just more difficult. It requires effort to be expended on care and compassion for their concerns about lifestyle change. You shouldn't try to force this on other people. But you, as a single young healthy guy, have no excuse not to do this, honestly. And as a side effect of spending so little money, you're saving a handful of years of freedom every year, you're actually living a healthier life, and you're at least in the neighborhood of the global equitable burn rate."

"The global equitable – what?" he asks. "What's that?"

The Global Equitable Burn Rate

"Imagine you're in line at a buffet," I say. "You're near the front of the line, because you're a white American middle class guy. The table is piled with food. Everyone ahead of you in line is loading up their plates in a frenzy, some people even are getting wheelbarrows and shoveling stuff in. Got the picture?"

"Sure. Feeding frenzy at the buffet," he smiles. We've always been a sucker for buffets.

"Now look behind you," I say. "What do you see?"

His smile fades. "—Oh. I see about eight billion people, don't I."

I nod. "And you start to wonder if there is enough food for all of them, too. You start to ponder the ethical implications of taking more food than you really need."

"That's quite a metaphor," he says. "The food on the table represents global GDP, doesn't it."

"That's right," I say. "But it's not as simple as dividing global GDP by population and saying that's what's fair. Because the global economy is consuming resources at a rate that would take more than one earth to supply. There's actually *too much food* on the table. So the *sustainable* fair share of consumption is GDP divided by *the global human footprint, divided by population.*"

$$\text{Global Equitable Burn Rate} = \frac{\text{World GDP}}{\text{Overshoot} * \text{Population}}$$

$$\text{GEBR} = \frac{\$101.33 \text{ Trillion per year}}{1.7 \text{ Earths} * 8.1 \text{ Billion humans}}$$

$$\text{GEBR} = \$7,359$$
(per human, per Earth, per year)

"What is that number?" he asks.

"A little over seven thousand dollars a year," I say. "As far as calculations go, you can make all kinds of arguments against it. If everyone only spent seven grand, the economy would collapse. It doesn't take into account the impact of specific purchasing decisions, like taking a train vs flying. Seven thousand dollars consumes more in rural Ohio than it does in New York City." I wave my hand. "It's just a rough calculation, a guideline, not a precise moral mandate. It paints a picture of how ridiculously out of bounds the normal western lifestyle expectation is. The standard American lifestyle is not a few small eco-consumerist tweaks away from a sustainable civilization. Also, having this number in mind can help with eco-analysis paralysis."

"You mean like how people agonize over whether they should buy a stainless steel straw to drink out of rather than use disposable recycled paper ones?"

"Yeah," I say. "People agonize over tiny bullshit like that when they're blowing seventy a year like I was, flying to Bali for yoga retreats for a long weekend and burning a barrel of gasoline every weekend going to the mountains. The sustainable equitable consumption calculation is nice because it gives you something to aim for and you can focus on more important stuff than if your fucking toothbrush handle is made from ethically sourced bamboo or not."

"But does it matter?" he asks.

"What do you mean?"

"Will a few people reducing their consumption to the global equitable burn rate make a difference?"

"Of course not," I say. "That's not the point. The point is that learning how to build a good life that doesn't cost so much money is a prerequisite for becoming a post-consumer and blazing the path to the successor cultures that will, one way or another, consume no more than the carrying capacity of the earth and make space for people to live better lives. It's a way to deprogram consumer ideology in your own mind. It's a way to crowbar your way to economic freedom as quickly as possible. And, as someone who claims to be bothered by the fact that global civilization is in overshoot, it's a way of putting your money where your mouth is. It is, in other words, a matter of character. There's a whole bucket of reasons to do it and very few good ones not to."

How Long to Work For

He thinks this over. "So, how long do I do this for?"

I frown. "How long do you spend sustainably for?"

"No, I mean how long do I keep working while spending below ten thousand, earning five plus years of freedom every year."

"Oh. It's up to you. That's the magic of it. If you're enjoying yourself, you could work until you've got enough saved to never have to work again. That number is about thirty."

"Thirty? Thirty what?" he asks.

"If you save and invest thirty or so years of living expenses and learn the basics of personal finance, your money will probably never run out and you can consider money a solved problem. And then—well, and then you just do whatever you want. Any project you want, travel anywhere, work on anything, get involved in any organization or group. Become an activist, a writer, a traveler, a permaculture guru, join an ecovillage, become a monk, build furniture, make art, become an entrepreneur, whatever. Wherever your stoke and your values lead you.

"You could also work only a couple more years, save up a buffer of five to ten years living expenses, and then quit and hit the road, travel, try different things, explore the world, explore your options."

"But I'd still have to go back to work at some point if I did that," he says.

"You'd have to generate some more money in your life, yes. How difficult is it to earn seven to ten thousand dollars a year?"

He blinks. "I imagine it's not very difficult."

"It is not. You could take on interesting seasonal gigs. You could write books and they wouldn't have to sell a million copies to finance your life. You could sell courses on the internet. You could build a tiny house and sell it once a year. You could find thrift store furniture, fix it up nice, and flip it. Or you could get a real job, work for another couple years and save up thirty-ish years of expenses, and be done with earning money forever. There are a million easy ways to pay the bills when your cost of living is super low. That's another reason it's magic."

"Wait, what about health care? Insurance is super expensive, you forgot about that."

"When I earn above the government subsidy limit, I pay for my health insurance. When I earn below the subsidy limit, the government pays for my health insurance," I say.

"Isn't that like welfare? For poor people?"

I shrug. "I guess. I didn't design the American health insurance system, I just play the rules. My primary strategy is to live a very healthy lifestyle and avoid incurring health cost as much as possible. If that fails, I've got health insurance one way or the other, according to the rules of the system that someone else came up with. It just so happens that I spend so little money that I don't need to earn very much. Since I don't need to earn very much, I often fall into the group of people who get subsidized coverage. It seems dumb to work more to earn more money to pay for health coverage that the government would supply for free, particularly since I almost never actually incur significant costs to the system."

"What if the rules of the system changes?" he asks.

I frown at him. "Then I'll adapt. Obviously. Anyway, it's not like I'm ripping the system off in order to sit at home playing video games. My full time occupation is helping myself and others prepare for a destabilized future. It might not be an officially recognized role, but I'm fully engaged in the work of being useful to society. On my own terms. Also, since I'm spending so little, I'm consuming way fewer resources than your average first-worlder. My conscience is entirely clean on this one. If it bothers you, you'd have to figure out how to make enough money every year to qualify to pay for health insurance yourself. It doesn't make the strategy not work, it just makes it more of a pain in the ass. Do what you like."

"I'll have to think about that," he says.

What to Do with Your Accidental Pile of Money

"Wait, what do I do with all the savings?" he asks. "Do I just leave it in my savings account? Won't it just inflate away? That's a thing, right?"

"That's one of the skills you'll have to learn, how to manage your savings," I respond. "A common strategy is to keep a cash buffer of a few years and dump the rest in index funds of equities, bonds, and commodities."

He frowns. "How is that better than spending it on consuming stuff? Aren't I just passing the consumption on to corporations to do whatever they're doing with it?"

"When you buy a stock you aren't giving the company money to blow on more equipment. You're buying ownership from someone else. Stock ownership isn't revenue for a company. But, yeah, having your money in the markets is at minimum an investment in how the system works," I shrug. "You don't have to invest in the stock market. You have options.

"You can leave the money in your checking and savings account. Inflation will eat it, and the bank will use it as leverage to invest. So that's no better than putting it in the markets yourself, except the bank benefits instead of you.

"You can dump it into index funds, owning a little bit of, say, the S&P500. As long as the economy keeps doing what it has been doing, you will at minimum preserve your wealth over the long term and probably accrue a lot more, as long as you don't pull it out in a downturn.

"You can actively manage your portfolio and invest directly in companies that you think are doing good things in the world, or at least not invest in companies that are doing things you don't agree with.

"You can keep your money in really conservative vehicles like CDs, iBonds, Treasuries, and the like. You might preserve your wealth, but you might also lose out to inflation.

"You can take the cash out and keep it in a shoebox under your bed, hope you never get robbed, and watch inflation eat it.

"You can buy physical gold or silver and keep *that* in a shoebox under your bed, and hope you never get robbed, and maybe at least preserve the value of the cash.

"You can give all your surplus away and work forever.

"You can work only enough to cover a little bit into the future and never accumulate any significant surplus. So, you could work for only a couple months a year, every year. In this case you're still locked in to having to work, and if you lose the ability to work due to health issues you'll be hosed. So this method is either stupid or saintly. Or both.

"You can invest all of your surplus cash in tools, materials, and skill training.

"You can learn how to live with no or almost no money at all, like Daniel Suelo, Mark Boyle, or Robin Greenfield.

"Or you can do a bit of all of the above. Have some in the markets, in companies that you think aren't so bad. Bury some gold coins under a rock somewhere. Spend some money on tools and infrastructure, a permaculture place. Spend money on books and skills courses. Keep developing your skills and social networks so you need less and less money, work the skill ratchet until you could live off of two thousand, one thousand, no dollars a year, if you had to. Work seasonally. Build some passive income gigs that bring in just enough to live off a year. Give away the rest.

"It's up to you. Don't put any in the markets if it's too icky for you. The point is that the worst option is to keep working full time and blow all your money on dumb crap you don't need. The worst option is to stay locked in wage slave consumerism, with no freedom and no skills, whining about capitalism but not doing anything about it. Using the rules of the game to escape the game is the least-bad option I've come across. The approach I'm talking about is weighted towards pragmatism and increasing personal adaptive capability, not idealism."

"What do you do?" he asks.

"A bit of all of the above, for now," I say. "I have a retirement account and a brokerage account that I mostly have in index funds and I don't think about it much. I have some in cash, in CDs and iBonds and the like, so even if my retirement funds evaporate in a depression I have years of living expenses saved. I spend money on tools and building materials and books. I'm constantly working on increasing my skills to be able to solve problems with competence that I currently spend money to solve. I've got a side hustle that brings in a bit more income than I spend every year. I have the skills and relationships to do enough low-key handyman work to cover my living expenses locally if I wanted to. In other words, I put in some effort into 'solving' money and now I barely think about it. I do things that I am intrinsically motivated to do, that are aligned with my skills and interests, I spend a tiny amount of time managing my money, and it's simply there when I need it. It's on tap."

He blows out his breath. "This is crazy."

"No, it's really not," I say. "Working sixty hours a week for forty years to retire with a wrecked body and a domesticated soul to spend money on dumb crap that doesn't actually make you feel any better is crazy. Learning how to have a meaningful life on a tiny amount of money and then getting to do whatever you want is *abnormal,* yes, but it's the opposite of crazy. It's very, very not crazy."

"If it's so not crazy then why aren't more people doing it?" he asks.

"Because it is difficult," I say. "At first. It takes a big initial effort of will and self education to write a new script for yourself when there is a lot of social pressure to just go with the flow. You have to be very dissatisfied with the standard scripts and some people just aren't. Some people are fine with how things are going. Some people are unwilling to be a weirdo even if they understand that normal behavior is insane.

"Also it's outside of the current paradigm, and thinking outside of the paradigm is difficult. It doesn't occur to most people that this is even an option, that it is even possible. I *wanted* to think outside of the paradigm and I didn't know this was an option until I found Jacob's work. The actual actions aren't that difficult, really, once you do them a few times it starts to feel normal. What's actually difficult is expanding your thinking to realize what's possible, and then sticking with it despite social pressure to conform to consumer behavior. In retrospect it isn't very complicated: just figure out how to spend way below your income, save and manage your money, and hey presto your financial needs are taken care of forever. But spending so little of your income is so far outside of normal behavior it doesn't occur to most people as an option.

"Also, more people than you realize do this, they just don't advertise it. Very few people really understand this kind of lifestyle. If you tell normal people how much you spend or how little you have to work, they assume you're some kind of hobo and they make fun of you because they don't understand you. Or they assume you're a trust fundie. It's annoying to talk about it. So most people who live this way do it quietly."

"So, make some strategic moves to reduce expenses, do a No Buy Year to crowbar my way towards an equitable burn rate, steward the surplus, and get free in a short amount of time," he says. "Is that it then? We're done here? This is all I need to know?"

I grin at him. "Not even remotely."

Further Reading

For a first-principles mathematical model of how saving 85% of your income will result in financial independence in 5 years, see Chapter 7 of *Early Retirement Extreme*.

Adeney, Peter (2012, January 13). *The Shockingly Simple Math Behind Early Retirement.* https://www.mrmoneymustache.com/2012/01/13/the-shockingly-simple-math-behind-early-retirement/

https://portfoliocharts.com/

https://www.madfientist.com/

Big ERN, (2016, December 7). *The Ultimate Guide to Safe Withdrawal Rates – Part 1: Introduction.* https://earlyretirementnow.com/safe-withdrawal-rate-series/

Merkel, Jim. (2003). *Radical Simplicity: Small Footprints on a Finite Planet.* New Society Publishers.

Sundeen, Mark. (2012). *The Man Who Quit Money.* Riverhead Books.

Boyle, Mark. (2010). *The Moneyless Man: A Year of Freeconomic Living,* Oneworld Publications.

https://www.robingreenfield.org/

7. Throw Competence At It, Not Money

"The rain stopped. Let's go for a walk," I say.

"A walk? It's eleven thirty," he says.

"So?"

"There's a progress set going out by end of day tomorrow. I need to get in early to pick up the comments Steve left tonight."

"You're going in early to do work that Steve should have gotten to you days ago? For a progress set?" I shake my head. "What project is it for?"

"The Lily office retrofit."

I think for a second. "I don't even remember a Lily office retrofit. Come on. You'll never have a chance to talk with your future self again."

I grab his notebook from the table and lead us north and east into the residential neighborhoods of the Oakland hills.

Quality of Life is a Function of Skills

"There's something I don't get," he says. "You can go on the internet and look up the cost of living for different cities. There's a number that represents how expensive it is to live there, to achieve some basic level of quality of life. You seem to be saying that that those numbers don't mean anything. How does that make sense?"

"Those cost of living numbers aren't meaningless, but they're all assuming a similar basket of goods and a similar skill level. They assume everyone solves all of their problems with money. Under the standard assumptions of consumerism, the more you spend, the higher your quality of life. If your spending drops below some threshold, which varies by location, then your quality of life is considered unacceptably low. We're conditioned to think that quality of life is a function of how much money you spend."

"I know that money can't buy happiness," he says, "but below some threshold of spending it just isn't feasible to have a good life. You're just scraping by."

"Yes, but that threshold of spending is a function of location, personal circumstances and preferences, and *skills*. This is the fundamental difference between consumerism and post-consumerism. Under consumerism, you meet your needs by spending money. You spend money to get goods, entertainment, and experiences. Under post-consumerism, you embody the insight that there are more ways to meet your needs then spending money to get them. You can reduce the threshold below which your quality of life drops."

He frowns. "I'm not sure I understand."

"Here's an example: if you have the basic skills of cooking tasty food at home from simple, inexpensive ingredients, you can spend far less on food and have a higher quality of life because the food is going to be healthier and, often, tastier. If you know even a little bit about how to store bulk staples, you can have a pantry that would last you a few months if services got disrupted. Now you're not just living at a lower cost of living for a higher quality of life, your household is more resilient.

"I used to spend at least a thousand dollars a month on food and alcohol for just myself. Now I spend two hundred or less and my food related quality of life is higher because I'm healthier, I get satisfaction out of learning to cook, and I feel better knowing that if something happened to the grocery stores I've got three months of food in my pantry.

"Poverty is the state of not having enough resources to meet your needs. If you can figure out how to meet your needs on less than ten thousand dollars, then you aren't in poverty even if technically you spend below the poverty line.

"Under consumerism, your quality of life is purely a function of how much money you can spend. The more money you can spend, the more stuff you can consume, and the better your life is. That's the claim.

"But I'm not playing that game anymore. The game I'm playing has a lot of different names: post-consumerism, degrowth, solarpunk, or voluntary simplicity are the most common ones. This other game claims that the good life is a function of money *as well as* the depth and breadth of your competence in multiple domains. This is obviously true but we lose sight of it. It's difficult to realize just how little money you actually need to live a good life if you possess adequate skills."

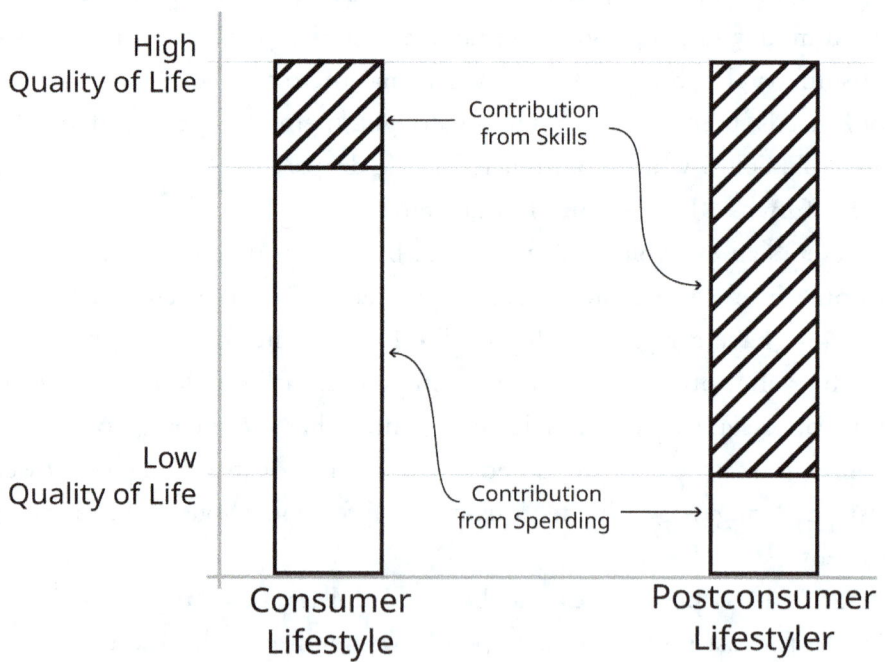

The Commodification of Human Experience

"Skills," he says flatly. "Like, cooking. And what else, how to change a flat tire? How to wire an electrical socket?"

I nod. "Sure, those help. The basic skills related to your needs for shelter, food, staying warm and dry, staying clean and healthy and safe. Also skills related to your social and psychological needs, mental health, wisdom, your spiritual needs, your needs for play and curiosity and meaning and fulfillment. All of them. We're conditioned from birth to assume that you need money to secure these needs. Money is our hammer, and our needs as complex human beings look like a bunch of nails."

He frowns. I continue.

"If your bike breaks, how do you fix it?"

"I drop it off at the bike shop."

"If your room is too cold, how do you fix it?"

"I buy a space heater."

"If your pants get a hole in them, how do you solve that?"

"I buy a new pair of pants." He's getting heated again. Good, I might actually be able to use it now.

"If you're feeling ungrounded, overwhelmed, and tight as a drum, how do you solve that?"

"I go to a yoga class."

"Why don't you fix your bike yourself, or build a passive solar house for yourself, or mend your own clothes, or do yoga poses by yourself or with friends in your living room or at a park?"

"Because I don't have time for that, I work!" he says hotly.

I throw my hands up in the air. "Exactly! No one has time for that because everyone is too busy working! You're only good at doing whatever it is you do at work, and you pay for everything else because that's the most efficient use of your time. And that is exactly the way the system wants it. The system *wants* everyone to specialize and to have to pay other specialists to do everything else for them, because that maximizes the amount of money getting sloshed around the economy.

Consumer capitalism wants to own our competencies. It wants us to be feeble, because feeble people are commodities. Consumerism wants *all work* to be in the formal economy, and *no work* to be in the informal economy. The informal economy is an untapped source of wealth that can be exploited and funneled up to–"

I'm ranting again. I chop my hand through the air and take a breath.

"Basically everyone in the western world has so few skills that they need to spend something like seventy thousand a year just to feel adequate about themselves," I say. "Money is how people are taught to survive this world. They don't have the skills to live well on less than that. That's the point here. Quality of life is in reality a function of money *and skills.* And most people have almost no skills, because the logic of the system has been making each generation less competent than the one before it for a long time. Human competence is almost entirely commodified."

The Fallacy of Comparative Advantage

"Well, fine," he says, "but the whole point of specialization is that you can earn money at a more efficient rate than you spend it. Let's say I earn $30/hr. Fixing my bike will take me two hours. That's sixty bucks of my time. If I can have the shop do it for no more than fifty dollars, that's a no-brainer. Just drop it off at the shop and I've got more time to myself, or to work on decarbonizing the built environment."

"Ah yes, the fallacy of comparative advantage," I say. "That holds up if time and money are the only things being optimized for. It's the logic of internalized consumerism."

"What do you mean?" he asks.

"Having other people take care of basic stuff like fixing your bike makes you *dependent.* Spending money to have other people solve your problems makes you need to earn money to solve your problems. It makes you less resilient and less self sufficient. Which is fine if you don't care about being resilient and self sufficient, but this isn't an ideal century to hold that attitude."

"But there's a catch-22," he says. "In order to work less, I need a bunch of skills. But in order to learn and use those skills, I need to work less."

I wave my hand. "The low hanging fruit don't take much time to learn. You crowbar the easy wins while still working full time, which gets you spending significantly less than you earn, and you save up a buffer. You can use that buffer later to buy yourself more time to learn more. Skill acquisition is very boot-strappable, especially for a single dude with no dependents."

"So, what, just start going out and learning a bunch of random skills?" he asks.

"I recommend being strategic about it," I say. "You can get lost in the abstract idea of packing on new skills, but if it's all underwater basket-weaving it's not going to do you much good."

How to Acquire Skills

"So how do I approach it, then?"

"One way is to think of skill acquisition in three categories: fundamentals, vocation, and stoke."

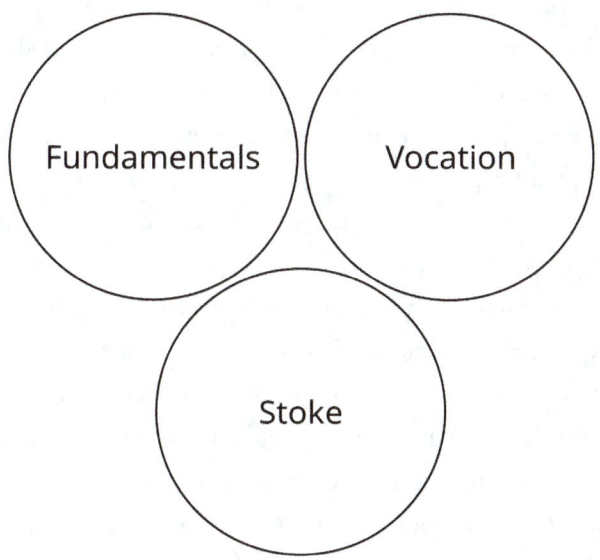

Fundamental Skills

"Start with the fundamentals, your basic human needs. You need to eat, sleep, stay warm and dry, get around, get dressed, talk to people, be healthy, and organize your money. We already talked about the emergency escape skills you can employ with food and shelter, right?"

"Sort of," he says. "We mostly talked about how to go without a bunch of stuff to cut expenses."

"Learning to go without every once in a while is a useful skill, too. Our culture wants us to think that the second we have a desire for something we're supposed to go out and fulfill it like entitled brats.

"Anyways, cutting out a bunch of stuff to get expenses low immediately is step one of the crowbar method. That strategy is to do whatever is necessary to start earning as much freedom as quickly as possible and to force yourself to learn alternative methods for solving your problems. But that's just the first step. The second step is to learn the skills necessary to have a high quality of life without spending a lot of money to get it.

"For example, right now you eat out a lot. If you just stop eating out cold turkey, the tastiness of the food you eat is going to decrease because you're not a very good cook, right? But with a little effort, you can learn to make your own cooking a lot tastier. That's a skill. So you've cut your cost, invested a little time in increasing your cooking skill, and you can bring your quality of life right back up to where it was when you were eating out all the time. But your quality of life will actually be higher, because you'll be eating healthier due to higher quality ingredients, and you'll feel good because you're more competent now and humans really like being competent at stuff, you've made yourself more attractive on the dating market – there are a lot of benefits.

"When it comes to fundamentals and how to approach skill acquisition, there's a balance of strategic thinking and interest to take into account. Don't turn it into drudgery. Let your interest guide you. What are your favorite foods from restaurants? Learn to make those from scratch. Can you make a burrito taste as good as an El Faralito burrito? Can you make a lasagna that's so good people invite you to their parties so you'll bring it? Can you make a dinner for twelve on short notice? Can you drop into any household and make something tasty from whatever they happen to have in the pantry, as appreciation for hosting you? Can you cook a steak on a grill? Do you know how to store staples for many months, so if there's some kind of disruption in the food supply chain you won't be in a panic? Food is an endless arena for skill development.

"You've got to sleep and keep your stuff somewhere. What form of shelter makes you most excited? Do you really want to live in a 1950s bungalow for $2,100 a month or do you want to find a cool warehouse space for $450 that you can build out yourself and be surrounded by interesting people creating interesting things? What about building a tiny house in someone's backyard, paying only $200 in rent and owning your own home that you can move somewhere else whenever you feel like it? Do you like living in a space that looks like it was decorated by a colorblind electrical engineer, or do you want to learn some basics of interior styling and make it soothing, beautiful, inspiring, reflective of your values?

"You've got to get around, but you're actually not a very good bike mechanic, which is weird considering you call yourself a mechanical engineer. Learn everything about it, make sure it's operating efficiently and that your biomechanics are on point. Does it make sense to get a bike that could handle more cargo and that you could use to go on overnight bike trips instead of renting a car for? Build one out of parts. If at some point car ownership makes sense, buying an older diesel vehicle and learning to keep it running and brew your own biodiesel out of waste vegetable oil sounds fun.

"Everybody has to put clothes on. You dress okay, but why not dress excellently? I don't mean wear a suit, I mean why not learn about clothing, learn to do simple repairs to keep up your stuff, learn how to pick out durable and timeless pieces, and maybe even learn what colors go with your skin tone, what hues make your eyes pop, how you can subtly and effectively communicate with how you dress yourself?

"Every two weeks money gets dumped into your checking account. Just leaving it there to lose value to inflation is the second stupidest thing you can do with it. Where should you keep a liquid emergency stash? Should you open a brokerage account? If so, what should your asset allocation be? What is the current interest rate environment like, and what does that imply for how you should manage your money? What are the most common mistakes that people make with their money, and how can you avoid them? Can you invest your money sustainably? Is that even a thing? How can you manage your money so that you never have money problems that you don't see coming a mile away?

"You spend time with friends, and your friends are incredible people. How else can you spend high quality time with them? Can you learn to get good at coming up with ideas for things to do, organizing events, initiating group trips? There are so many things you can do to build and strengthen relationships, from simple things like sending people notes to getting more intentional about inviting people to things to learning to become a good listener.

"The basic day to day stuff is a rich and rewarding place to begin with internalizing post-consumerism. Learning new skills takes effort, but these are all things you have to do anyway so you can incorporate skill acquisition into your daily life. And the more time you spend on the fundamentals, the more your cost of living comes down, the more freedom you earn every paycheck, the more resilient your household is, and the higher your quality of life becomes."

Vocation

"Another category is vocation, or your life's work or purpose, what you do to show up in society and provide value and, usually, earn some income. It's really important to grasp what I mean here by the word 'vocation'. A vocation is more than just a job, in fact a vocation could have nothing at all to do with a job. A vocation is something you feel called to do, something you feel strong purposeful alignment with.

Finding your true vocation is difficult, and so its more of a process of educated guesses and iterative searching, but we'll get into that later.

"For the purposes of skill development it doesn't really matter if you know exactly what your vocation is or not. Your vocation is often discovered by educated trial and error, experimentation and improvisation. So even if you're not sure what your vocation is there are a lot of skills that will support the journey. Writing, public speaking, emotional intelligence, task organization and project management, search and analysis, the ability to focus and concentrate, and proficiency with whatever technologies or workflows are relevant to your current work are all fine skills to work on.

"There's basically no work that doesn't involve writing, and most people suck at writing. It's pretty easy to become an above average writer. Read Strunk and White, read good writing, and actually take the time to revise your own writing a few times before sending it even if it is just an email.

"The only thing people suck at worse than writing is public speaking. Becoming a halfway decent public speaker is such a slam dunk, because since most people suck at it so hard they *love* it when someone is good at it. This is mostly about reps, getting time in. Join Toastmasters, offer to give lunchtime presentations at work, be proactive about giving talks at conferences and the like. And then put in a lot of effort to make them as good as possible. Record yourself and study your own behavior. Study really good public speakers. When you have to sit through a terrible public speaker, study them. Why do they suck so hard? What about what they're doing makes the experience horrible for everyone?

"The ability to focus and concentrate is another no-brainer. Most people are distracted to the point of effective stupidity. They aren't actually stupid people but when they're so distracted that they only use a small bit of their brains a small amount of the time they might as well be. Focus is a superpower. Develop advanced skills of focus and concentration.

"The rest of this category is the specifics of your vocations. Put in the time and effort to study, train, and practice. Why should anyone know more about your fields than you? It's not that difficult to read all of the books about your fields of interest. Almost no one does this but all it takes is consistent effort over time."

"What's an example of this?" he asks.

"Your current vocations are sustainable engineering of the built environment and building information modeling, right?" I ask. He nods. "For starters, you should read every book even kind of related to both of those fields. You should find mentors and peers who know more than you and learn from them. You should seek niches of arcane knowledge related to those fields, and become known as a subject matter expert. As soon as you can you should start teaching what you know, because teaching is like dumping gasoline on the learning process."

He shakes his head. "I mean, yeah, but this is a lot."

"Well, yeah," I say. "What else are you here for? To watch Netflix and fart around? I'm not saying that you have to become obsessed with work. I'm saying that you should identify what you think you care about and invest effort in it. If you find yourself doing things you don't care about, you should invest effort in figuring out how to stop doing those things. The universe rewards going deep on things you care about."

Stoke-Directed Skills

"Speaking of, the third category is anything you're intrinsically motivated to do, stuff that you want to do for its own sake. This can be anything. Yoga, welding, programming, writing, gardening, improv, organizing dinner parties or street protests, photography, dancing, painting, climbing – whatever. The idea is to take what you're interested in and then take a craft approach to it. Don't turn it into a job or an obligation, but let yourself get obsessed with it and get really good at it. Getting really good at stuff is fun." I shrug. "There really isn't much more to say about this category. The main skill here is the meta-skill of relearning how to play and approach things with authentic curiosity.

"So fundamentals, vocation, and stoke. Those are the three categories I think about in terms of skill acquisition. A given activity could be all three, or two, right? Most are at least two. You might learn that you really love cooking, and so that is both a fundamental skill and a stoke skill. Your 3d modeling stuff is both life's-work and stoke. Building a tiny house is an expression of the fundamental need for shelter, the stoke of 3d modeling and design and swinging a hammer, and your life's work of making the built environment suck less. That's all three categories.

"The secret to the good life is to overlap stoke as much as possible with the other two categories, in particular vocation. People get really good at what they're intrinsically motivated to do, so paying close attention to where stoke overlaps your guesses at vocation is critical."

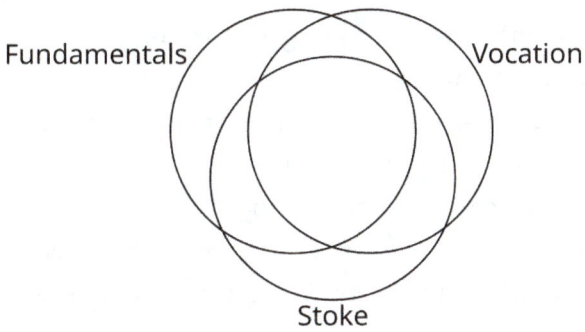

"What's the end game with all this skill acquisition? When do I know I've learned enough?" he asks.

I laugh. "You'll never learn enough, that's the best part. It's an infinite game. The point of skill acquisition is that skill acquisition is fun, meaningful, and a very natural thing for a human being to do. Skill development isn't a goal, it's a process that you won't want to stop. Once you get a solid practice of skill acquisition integrated into your lifestyle the idea of ever 'stopping' won't make any sense to you. It'll just be your way of life. Incidentally, this process will make your cost of living very low, it will make your household very resilient, and it will almost certainly make you a valuable contributing member of the unfolding future society that is rising out of the mess of the current arrangement.

"Developing a relationship with skill development that works for you is an important part of all of this. The crowbar method is all well and good, but it's possible to get trapped in it, to become obsessed with spending very little and getting stuck in a scarcity mindset. That's not post-consumerism, that's just the flip side of the consumerism coin. The crowbar method creates a pocket of non-consumerism in your life that you can use to figure out alternative ways of directing your life. Developing a personalized set of skills that you can use to engage with the world in a productive, creative, unique way is how you simply leave the logic of consumerism behind you. It's how you craft a lifestyle that is specifically yours and that you love to inhabit."

He mulls this over. "Sounds self-centered."

I sigh. "You're suspicious of any behavior that doesn't hurt. You think that the "right" things to do involve sacrifice and personal pain, to the point that you instinctively avoid anything that feels good. This isn't just wrong, it's dumb. It makes you avoid things that you're actually best suited to. Engaging in enjoyable activity is a hack for high performance due to the mechanisms of intrinsic motivation that we already talked about. *Avoiding* enjoyable activity is a great way to nerf yourself. The world doesn't need more martyrs, dragging themselves through their dreary pain-filled lives, only able to get off on how put-upon they feel. The world needs people with the spark of life in them, people who are pursuing the best, most actualized versions of themselves. Avoiding anything that feels good is a great way to sabotage your life. Get over yourself, let yourself discover what you actually enjoy and are good at, and double down on that. Use stoke instead of pain as your north star. You'll be surprised how far that gets you."

Further Reading

Another model for thinking about skill acquisition is to be a jack of all trades, master of some. Jacob proposed a rough target of one 10,000hr 'specialty', 3-5 3,000hr areas of expertise, and many 300hr interests. The hour representing amount of time invested in skill acquisition.

Nate Hagens, interview with Vicki Robin, *The Great Simplification: Vicki Robin "Money and Life's Energy,"* podcast audio, June 1, 2022, https://www.thegreatsimplification.com/episode/21-vicki-robin

One thing that trips people up is they think the good life is a "happy" one. But happiness is just one value, one possible dimension of a good life, and different people have different values. For some people it is important to have a happy life. For others it is important to have a meaningful or purposeful life. Yet others are more interested in having a psychologically rich life. The list goes on (satisfaction, contentedness, and pleasure are others that come to mind). Some of these life experience values act counter to each other – psychological richness often demands activities that will reduce your pleasure or happiness.

Digging into the literature on what constitutes the good life is useful primarily because it makes it clear that the good life is a choose your own adventure.

Easterlin, R.A., O'Connor, K.J. (2022). *The Easterlin Paradox.* In: Zimmermann, K.F. (eds) Handbook of Labor, Human Resources and Population Economics. Springer, Cham. https://doi.org/10.1007/978-3-319-57365-6_184-2

Oishi, Shigehiro, Westgate, Erin C. (2022) *A Psychologically Rich Life: Beyond Happiness and Meaning.* American Psychological Association. https://doi.org/10.1037/rev0000317

It's important not to get the concept of Standard of Living confused with the concept of Quality of Life. *"WHO defines Quality of Life as an individual's perception of their position in life in the context of the culture and value systems in which they live and in relation to their goals, expectations, standards and concerns."*

WHOQOL: Measuring Quality of Life. World Health Organization. https://www.who.int/toolkits/whoqol. Retrieved September 9, 2024.

Standard of Living has to do with qualitative measures like income, inflation, access to employment opportunities, and the like. Modern culture has perversely massively increased the average first world Standard of Living while making Quality of Life more difficult by constantly barraging people with messages that their position in life is actually lacking, causing them to work more and stress more sprinting on the hedonic treadmill.

Hayes, Shannon. (2010) *Radical Homemakers: Reclaiming Domesticity from a Consumer Culture.* Left to Write Press.

Tremayne, Wendy Jehanara. (2013). *The Good Life Lab: Radical Experiments in Hands-On Living.* Storey Publishing, LLC.

I didn't talk about *how* to acquire new skills because that is such an enormous topic that no treatment I could give it would be close to even scratching the surface. These books are a good place to start:

Ahrens, Sonke. (2022). *How to Take Smart Notes: One Simple Technique to Boost Writing, Learning and Thinking*. Sonke Ahrens.

Sterner, Thomas M. (2012). *The Practicing Mind: Developing Focus and Discipline in Your Life*. New World Library.

Waitzkin, Josh. (2008). *The Art of Learning: An Inner Journey to Optimal Performance*. Free Press.

Young, Scott. (2019). *Ultralearning: Accelerate Your Career, Master Hard Skills and Outsmart the Competition*. Harper Collins UK.

Lobenstine, Margaret. (2013). *Renaissance Soul: How to Make Your Passions Your Life*. The Experiment Publishing.

Epstein, David. (2021). *Range: Why Generalists Triumph in a Specialized World*. Riverhead Books.

8. How To Think About Everything At Once

Thus, to increase effectiveness, the focus must be on improving on the strategy rather than improving on the tactics. Rather than using better tactics to reach goals, the goal-setting method must become better.
--Jacob Lund Fisker

"Okay," he says. "I crowbar my expenses down quickly, and then I focus on skill acquisition to improve my quality of life, increase resilience, drop cost of living even further, and tap into a stoke-fueled highly actualized life. That sounds simple enough when I say it like that, but it feels like a lot to hold in my head. It feels like I'm trying to hold more and more objects in my arms and you keep adding things. How do I keep it all straight?"

I nod. "You've got to learn the trick of thinking about everything all at once."

He scowls at me. "That doesn't sound possible."

"It isn't. That's why I said it's a trick. It's a stack of cognitive tools that allow you to go up a level in thinking. You need to go from thinking about the *components* of your life to *the relationship between components* of your life. When you do this, you begin to think of your life as a whole system. But you're in luck, I can explain it to you."

He sighs. "Of course you can."

"How do most people think about their lives?" I say.

"*Do* most people think about their lives?" he says. "I was under the impression that most people are just playing whack-a-mole, or tetris."

"Right," I say. "They're barely able to keep up with their problems as they come, and so they mostly just do what people around them do. They go to college, or they don't. They get a job, and a car, and a house, because that's mostly what they see people around them doing. A lot of people don't really think about their lives at all, as far as I can tell. They just absorb the rules and goals of people around them who are doing the same thing. It's a big consumerist circle-jerk, really.

"Some people get ahead of the pack a little and actually think about what they do want, but they think about things in isolation. They think about what kind of career, house, hobbies, or car really defines them as a person. But they don't think about the relationships between these things. They just sort of pick things off the shelf that look interesting. As a result, a lot of their behaviors work against each other. They want a job downtown, but they also want a house in the country, so they spend three hours in traffic every day commuting. They don't see how they're responsible for the consequences of their own decisions. They think sitting in traffic for seven hundred and twenty hours a year is nothing they have any control over.

"What you need to learn is how to think about your life *as a system*. You need to learn how to see the emergent effects and consequences of your actions, and ultimately how to construct a system that works the way you want. Most people's lives require an enormous amount of resources to run and they're not actually doing the things they really want to do. The amount of friction and waste in their lives is insane. And they wonder why they are stressed. On top of that, their lives are fragile. If any little thing goes wrong, either internally or in the world around them, the whole thing falls apart. By learning to think about your life like a system you will reduce friction and waste, and you'll create a life that is very resilient to disruption *and* you'll be able to build momentum towards the kind of life that you actually want to live. The aim is to get all of the parts of your life to fit together, to form a cohesive whole."

"Okay. How do I do that?" he asks.

"Disassembly and then reassembly," I say. "First, take everything apart and spread it out so you can see it. You need to understand the inputs and outputs of each component of your life, and what the negative and positive side effects are. Then you can start looking at groups of components, and seeing how they interact. The outputs from some components might be able to connect to the inputs of others. Some activities create friction for other activities. You start to notice where there is conflict in your actions and where there is cohesion. At a certain point you are able to think at the level of your whole life as a system, rather than component by component. At that level things get interesting and weird. You are able to make decisions that nudge your *whole life system* in the direction of closer alignment with your values and desires. Coherence goes up, friction goes down. The activity is less like building or operating a machine and more like gardening. Permaculture is actually a good metaphor for what the activity of running your life as a system is like. Lots of observation, intuition, and making small tweaks and observing the result."

"I'm quite sure I'm more lost than I was a minute ago," he says.

"We'll break it down," I say. "The first step is decomposition – learning to analyze your life piece by piece. What's something you do?" I pull the notebook out of my pocket and poise a pen over it.

Decomposition

"Something I do?" he asks.

"Some activity you engage in on a regular basis, anything."

"I mountain bike," he says.

"You *downhill* mountain bike," I correct him. "What do you get out of downhill mountain biking? Why do you do it?"

"It's fun."

"Be more specific."

He furrows his brow in concentration. "I drop into flow when the risks are high enough that I'm focused and the difficulty is challenging but not way over my head."

I nod as I scribble in the notebook. "Okay. We'll say that *flow* is the goal. Are there any other benefits of downhill mountain biking?"

He thinks for a second. "It's physical so it keeps me in shape. I spend time out in the woods. I spend time with friends, particularly when we go on weekend camping and biking trips."

"Okay, so these are the desirable benefits of downhill mountain biking," I say and show him my sketch. *DH MTB* is circled and *Flow* is to the right of it, connected with a line. There are lines above that line pointing to *exercise, time outdoors,* and *social.*

"Now, what are some undesirable outcomes of downhill mountain biking?"

"It costs money. Parts break. The bikes are expensive."

I nod, writing. "What else might cost money?"

"Hospital bills. That's another undesirable effect, I guess, the risk of breaking a bone or getting blunt head trauma is fairly high."

"Yep," I say. "Anything else?"

"I can't think of anything."

"Is it easy to downhill mountain bike if you live in the city and don't have a car?" I prompt him.

"Oh, right. No, I go with friends who have cars and we split gas costs. Otherwise I'd need my own car."

"Okay, that's a good set." I show him the sketch which now has arrows coming out and down to the right labeled *risk of injury, expensive,* and *car dependent.*

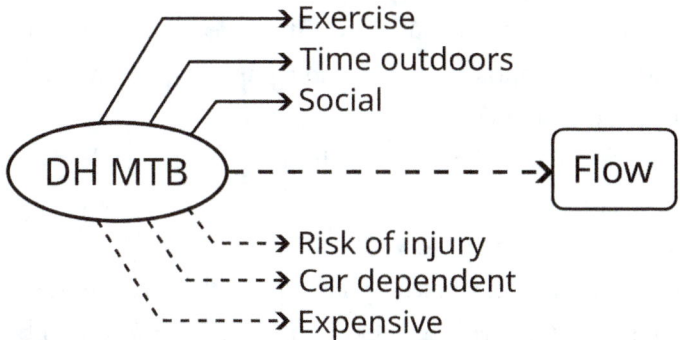

"All right," he says, and shrugs. "So I have this sketch of mountain biking. What do I do with it?"

"The most fundamental lesson here is to understand what it is you want," I say. "Is mountain biking what you want?"

He squints at me like I'm asking a very simple question. "Yes, duh. Mountain biking is fun and results in flow and all those other things."

"Is mountain biking *itself* the thing you like? Is there some ineffable, irreducible quality to the activity of mountain biking?" I tap my finger on the positive benefits I sketched earlier. "Or is it, in point of fact, effable?"

"Oh. You're suggesting that mountain biking isn't the point," he says. "Flow, exercise, outdoors, and time with friends are what I actually want. Mountain biking is just the delivery mechanism for those things."

"Mountain biking is *a* delivery mechanism for those things. Yes," I say, and tap the negative effects. "And this particular delivery mechanism costs you these things."

He frowns at me, suddenly suspicious. "Are you saying I shouldn't downhill mountain bike?"

"No. I'm saying you should understand what it is you actually want, how you're getting it, and what it costs. I'm not here to tell you what decisions to make. I'm trying to help you be able to make better decisions on your own. This exercise takes some effort when you first start doing it, but eventually you do it automatically."

"Let me do one," he says. "Climbing."

"Okay," I say, and ready the pen over the notebook. "Go ahead."

"I do it for the same reason: flow. Other positives are time outdoors, exercise, and deep bonds with climbing partners. Negatives are risk of injury and car dependence."

I look up from my sketch. "Is climbing as dependent on a car as mountain biking?"

"It's pretty similar," he says.

"Yes, but climbing gear takes up less space than a bike. It's a lot easier to catch a bus or hitch a ride as a climber than as a mountain biker."

"Okay, true," he admits. "Another negative is that climbing gear costs money. But once you've got the gear there isn't as high an ongoing cost as with mountain biking. So climbing generally costs less than downhill mountain biking."

I show him the sketch and he nods.

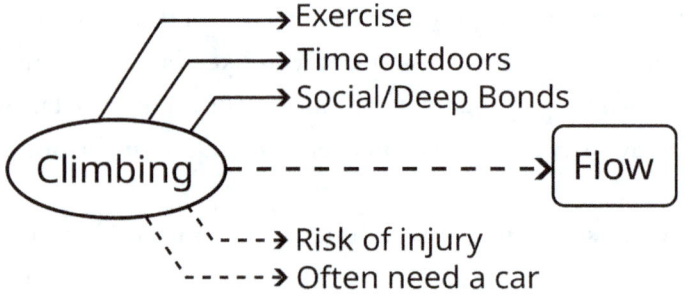

"Do you notice anything looking at the two activities?"

"They have similar benefits but climbing has fewer negative effects. So, what, I should drop mountain biking and only climb?"

I hold up my hands. "No, again, this is just about being able to see what's going on in your life so you can make better decisions. Having both mountain biking and climbing in your life might be perfectly fine right now. But maybe in the future your life system changes and holding both of these activities in your life begins to cause friction or tension. This kind of exercise can help you think that situation through. Here, look."

I quickly sketch another diagram and show it to him. The activity is

Own a car, with a goal of *travel long distances*. Positive effects are *travel autonomy* and *status*. Negative effects are *expensive, polluting, risk of death,* and *stressful*. "This is the normal way to solve the problem of covering long distances. But there are others."

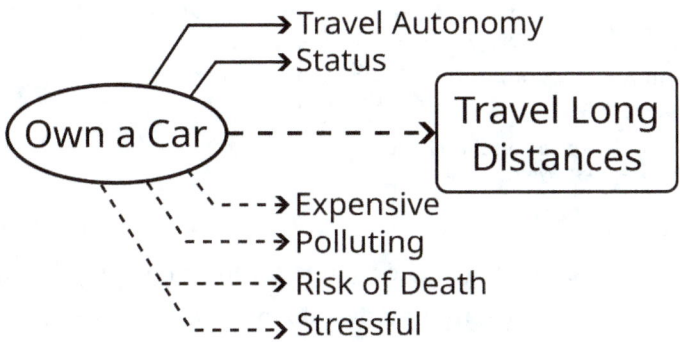

I sketch another diagram and show it to him. The activity is *hitchhiking*, with positive effects of *novel experiences, meet interesting people,* and *cover long distances*. Negative effects are *uncertain schedule/takes longer* and *risk of encountering dangerous weirdos*.

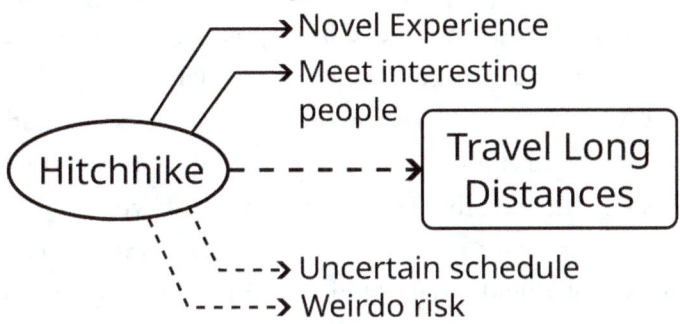

He looks at it and shrugs. "Okay."

"Look at all four sketches together. Combine hitchhiking with climbing and you've mitigated the negative effects and costs of car ownership while producing more positive benefits, such as novel experiences."

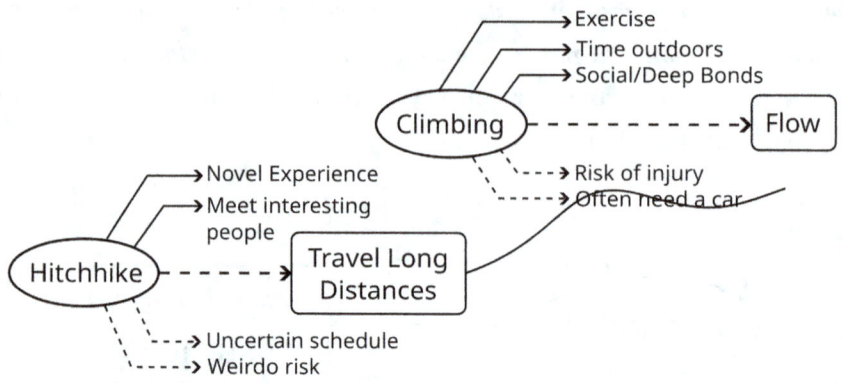

"Huh," he says, looking at the sketch. "And hitchhiking is a node that doesn't plug in well to mountain biking, because nobody picks up hitchhikers with bikes."

"Right. What we're doing here is analyzing nodes all around a theme. It started with thinking about activities you enjoy like mountain biking and climbing. We realized that covering long distances to get to the trail or the crag is a common requirement for these activities. And then we started looking at and analyzing different ways of solving the 'cover long distances' problem. And since we're listing out the positive and negative side effects we can start to get a sense for which solutions might work best for us. Owning a car is certainly the most convenient solution, but it has a lot of downsides and it lacks some of the positive benefits, like having novel experiences, that the other solutions have.

"If it's very important to you to be a serious climber then owning a car or a van is probably the right choice. But if climbing is just a delivery mechanism for challenge, being outdoors, bonding with people, and having novel experiences, then some of these other solutions to covering long distances might actually fit your life better than owning a car, even though they're less convenient. Riding your bike a hundred miles to the crag is way more interesting, challenging, and novel than driving a car. So is hitchhiking."

"Hitchhiking or bikepacking to a climb is a dumb idea if the important thing is to climb a lot," he says. "But if the point is to have interesting and challenging experiences, then they're a better fit. Yeah, that makes sense."

I nod. "And if one of your aims is to have an interesting life, you're going to want to maximize autonomy. The less money you spend, the less you have to work. Car ownership is expensive and not at all interesting. So car ownership would work against what you actually want out of life."

"But also," he looks at the sketch again, "moving someplace that is a within a few miles of decent mountain biking trails would eliminate the necessity of covering long distances, at least for mountain biking."

"Absolutely. And you could run these analyses on different potential locations to move. These sketches are a powerful tool," I tap the notebook. "It's like disassembling the parts of your life and spreading them out on the table so you can actually see everything at once. You want to spend a fair amount of time doing this level of analysis on everything. As many actions and goals in your life as you can think of."

"So do you have hundreds of these sketches tacked to your wall like a psycho?" he says.

"No," I say. "The sketches themselves aren't actually useful. *Sketching them* trained me to see connections between and consequences of my actions and goals in a clearer way. These sketches are training wheels. Eventually you will do this automatically and you won't need to sketch it out. I don't need a pen and paper and a calculator to know that cooking at home vastly outperforms eating out at a restaurant for all effects that I care about, or that car ownership has to provide a huge benefit to outweigh the significant negative effects."

"I still don't see what this has to do with systems thinking, though," he says. "This seems like a narrowing of focus."

"You have to learn how to take things apart before you can put them back together," I say. "We already started to do that when we began looking at how well car ownership, hitchhiking, or bikepacking fits with mountain biking or climbing activities. Once you've pulled things apart it is a natural step to re-combine them in novel ways. This is really the heart of it. Most people design their lives in the same way they order food at a restaurant. They look at the menu and pick something. Or they let someone else order for them.

"What we're doing is taking control of our lives. Forget the menu. Look at the recipes for different dishes. Go find your own ingredients. And combine them in interesting ways to make dishes that you want. Be your own chef. It's not for everyone, but if you want autonomy and alignment, this is what you have to do."

Reassembly: Patterns of Composition

"The important thing to understand is that I'm not asking you to perform some monumental feat of cognitive insight. You don't have to be some kind of genius to make better decisions about your life. We're just not taught effective ways of thinking thoroughly about our lives. We all want to build cathedrals but we're handed beach toy shovels. You don't need to be any smarter than you are. You just need to upgrade your thinking habits, become comfortable with a new set of tools, and the results will build over time.

"Let's start at the most basic level and work up from there. The simplest approach to thinking about your life is to *not* think about it at all. Some people do things without any kind of conscious reasoning and they don't understand the relationship between actions and outcomes, cause and effect. They're thirsty, they drink a coke, they're surprised when they get diabetes. They're bored, they scroll tiktok, they're surprised when they find themselves incapable of following a conversation that involves complete sentences. It's a very unconscious and unintentional approach to life."

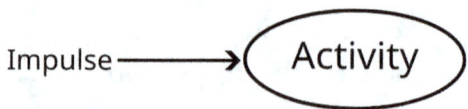

"Other people do actually think about what they want, and they work backwards to simple activities that will get them to their goals. They want to get ripped, so they join a gym. They want a big house, so they work a lot of overtime. They want to be healthy, so they eat salads and stop drinking soda. They formulate a desired outcome and then come up with a plan to realize that outcome. It's an improvement over an essentially unconscious planning methodology, but still rudimentary."

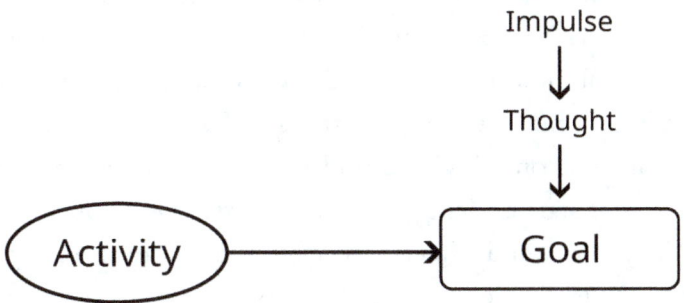

Effect Node Thinking

"Very few people think clearly about the positive and negative effects of their actions beyond their stated goal. That's what we just talked about with mountain biking and climbing. Mostly people only think about negative effects when they get hit in the face with them, but they might not even realize where it's coming from. Thinking about these effects ahead of time is rare. If you habituate this way of thinking you are doing better than the vast majority of people out there."

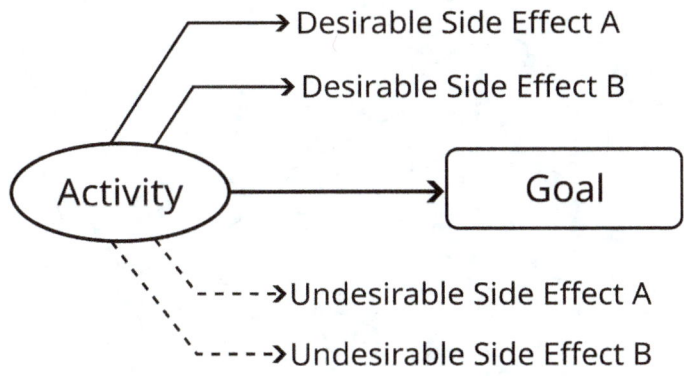

"It's important to get the hang of this step, of being able to see the positive and negative effects of individual actions. You've got to do it enough that it becomes automatic.

Node Cluster Thinking

"Once thinking through the positive and negative effects of your actions becomes effortless, you want to be able to think about a few behaviors or goals at a time, like we did with mountain biking, climbing, owning a car, and hitchhiking. This starts to happen naturally when you do a lot of analysis on individual nodes, because you lay them all out in front of you and start noticing patterns. At first you'll notice that it's just a jumble. The goals and effects don't have much relationship between them and the overall direction of all of your action-goal-effect nodes is high friction, no overall structure, a bit of a mess."

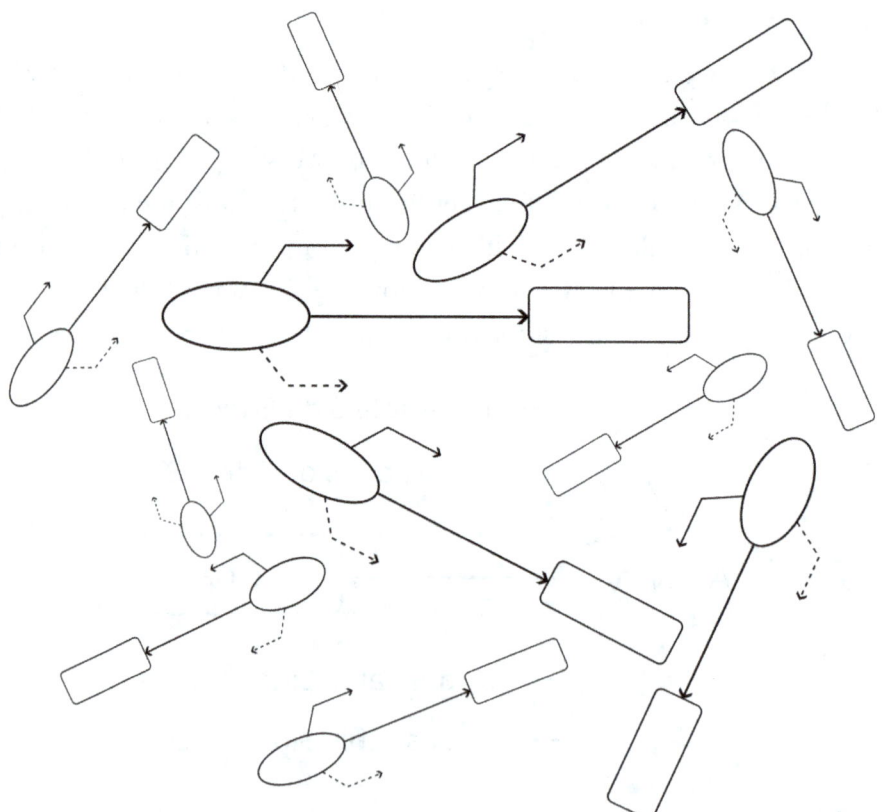

"It's at this stage that you realize how many of your actions are working against each other. It's a big step in terms of your thinking, because you've gone from thinking about actions and goals in isolation to thinking about—or at least *noticing*—the relationship between your sets of actions and goals. Once you can see this disorganization you can start organizing and aligning your goals so that they at least aren't pointing in opposite directions and working against each other.

"This step takes longer because it requires you to understand at a high level what you want your life to look like as a whole. The most difficult part of this process is simply understanding what it is you want as a unique individual. You've got to begin the process of teasing apart things you genuinely want for yourself and things that you *think* you want, but are in actuality programming from society, culture, parents, or friends. The reason most people's lives are a jumble of disconnected goals is because they don't have a clear and consistent idea of who they are and what they want.

"As you notice this you'll start to make more aligned decisions about your actions. You'll get a sense for where you're trying to go and start trimming actions that don't move you in that direction, and adopting behaviors that do. Your life as a system will start to look a lot more aligned. This isn't an overnight process. It's a lot like gardening."

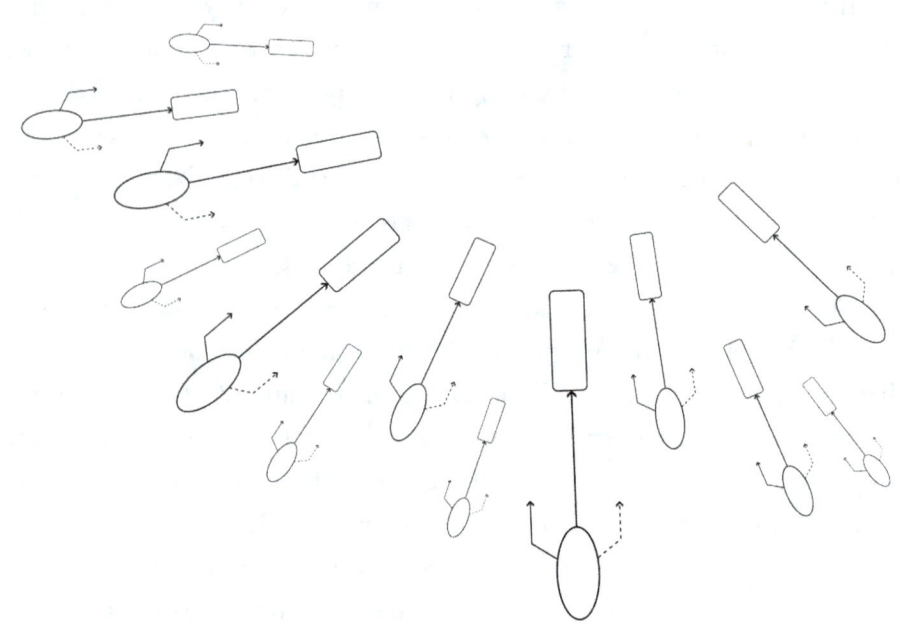

Webs of Goals Make Your Dreams Come True

"Most people make lists of goals," I say, "if they think about goals at all. What's the problem with a list of goals?"

He thinks, and looks at the notebook in my hand. "The goals on a list might have contradictory effects that are hard to see. If you just list them out it might not be obvious that *make partner at the firm* and *get really good at golf* is in conflict with *coach little league* and *win best dad ever award*. It's hard to see because the relationship between the goals isn't obvious."

"Yes. Thinking in terms of a web makes these relationships clearer. Also, a web is resilient. Break one strand and the web still holds together. You can suffer the destruction of a few nodes without catastrophe and have time to adapt to the new environment."

"Sure, unlike a chain, where if you cut one link the whole thing falls apart."

"Exactly. A chain is linear and every single link in the chain is absolutely critical to the integrity of the chain. The destruction of one link is catastrophic. A web is non-linear, so the destruction of any one node of a web is not catastrophic. There is no single element of it that, if cut, causes the whole thing to fail. You can cut one, two, even several parts of it and it'll still hold together."

"I get the picture, but I don't see how that applies to holistic thinking about my life," he says.

"Do you have any single points of failure in your life?" I say.

"Single point – uh."

"Almost *everything* in your life is a single point of failure," I say. "Again, work is the obvious example which we already talked about."

"If I lose my job, that cuts off my flow of money. I only have one source of money. That's what you mean, right?" he asks.

"That sort of thing, yes," I say. "As things stand you could get another similar kind of job easily enough. But what if you lost your job because the economy tanks and they don't need engineers anymore? What if you get in an accident and both your hands get cut off? What if you fall off your bike and get a serious concussion and can't look at computer screens for six months?"

"Those are all unlikely–"

"Unlikely but possible," I say, "and there are possible failure modes that you can't imagine. The point isn't to accurately predict specific disasters and avoid them. The point is to build a lifestyle that is generally robust to a wide variety of possible disasters, including ones you don't know about.

"The standard North American lifestyle is not very resilient because it's linear. For most people, if one component in their system breaks, their life falls apart. If they lose their job, they're hosed because everything depends on their paycheck. If their car breaks down, they can't get to work. If the grocery store doesn't have food in it, they're going to be hungry inside of three days. If the grid goes down, they're in the dark, freezing or overheating. Fragile. Always on the brink of disaster."

"But, I mean, there are institutions for that," he says. "Disaster relief organizations, debt relief – there are social safety nets out there."

"There are some, yes. The un-housed population of this country indicates that those nets have some significant holes in them, and big enough disasters regularly overwhelm relief organizations. The world I live in is no Mad Max post-apocalypse yet, at least not in North America, but it's becoming increasingly clear that things are becoming less stable. More volatile. It's getting increasingly stupider to assume that the services and resources we've counted on for a hundred years are going to save us. Part of systems thinking is to think in terms of how to not get ruined. You can't eat money if there are no groceries on the shelves to buy. The fact that you have less than a week's worth of food in your house makes my skin crawl."

"Okay, fine," he says. "But this still seems like a lot of complex cognitive effort just to make my life more resilient against potential disasters. Sure, that'd be nice, but I personally do have a lot of social safety nets so I'm not sure why I should put so much effort into this."

"Well, the other reason to internalize systems thinking is that all your dreams will come true," I say.

He blinks at me. "What do you mean your dreams will come true?" he says sharply. He seems upset with me. Odd.

"Your dreams will start to come true," I say. "Obviously, right? Except for the dumb ones. Look, a major reason that people are frustrated in how their lives are going is because their lives are set up to consume so many resources that they have to spend huge amounts of time just gathering resources, typically money, to keep the thing going. Also, since their life systems are fragile, they frequently experience little emergencies they have to scramble to fix. They don't have any time or resources available to purposefully direct the trajectory of their lives because they spend all their time scrambling to put out fires. This is stressful, and most people cope with the stress of this with numbing agents like alcohol, weed, driving fast, scrolling around on the internet, watching facile entertainments, whatever, which makes it even harder to get in control of their lives."

He pinches the bridge of his nose. "Yes, us normies have terribly delicate and stressful lives, you've mentioned that. Explain the part where your dreams come true if you internalize systems thinking."

"When you internalize systems thinking you decrease the amount of resources required to run your life, *and* you reduce the friction. This creates more space for you to think about your life, to simply *be*, without all of the running around, and to experiment with different activities. You tweak and tune as you go, observing the effect that different behaviors have on your overall experience of life. You remember, or discover, dreams and desires that you'd long forgotten about or didn't even know you had, and have the space to pursue them. You stop doing things that block your dreams. Your stress levels comes down and you don't need to use coping or numbing agents like alcohol as much, which improves the overall function of your life system because coping and numbing dissociates you from the experience of life and introduces other sources of friction. Over time your life activities converge on the imprint of interests, desires, and purpose that every human is born with, the grooves everyone has deep down. The closer you get to this imprint the stronger your attraction to it – it functions like a gravity well, the closer you get the stronger you feel it – and it eventually feels effortless to simply do the things you were made to do. Your life becomes consistently amazing."

"You could have led with that," he says. "You know that's way more compelling of a pitch than resilience, right?"

"I'll keep that in mind the next time I haunt a younger alternate-universe version of myself."

He shakes his head. "Explain how you internalize systems thinking."

A Life System Rugged Enough for Dream Chasing

"We want our lives to be resilient, because we want to maintain individual freedom-of-action, because we want to be able to chase stoke, fulfill our dreams, and generate adaptations to unfolding environment, because we want to contribute to creating successor cultures that will be a better fit for our future than the current arrangement. That's the motivation here, right?" I say.

"Right," he says. "Big picture, I want to be able to roll with the punches when they come and be light on my feet, so I don't waste my whole life just reacting to a volatile environment instead of playing an active role in shaping the future," he says. "I don't want to use my life to just fart around. I want to have an interesting life, sure, but also a life where I was able to do things that felt like they meant something. And," he says with emphasis, "I want all my dreams to come true."

"That's what everyone wants," I say. "The trouble with most people's approach is that they spend too much time daydreaming and not enough time building a life *system* that is robust. Their lives don't have the capacity to support their dreams. Some people YOLO after their dreams anyway and crash and burn when some little thing goes sideways. Other people don't even start because they know deep down that their lives are too fragile to withstand chasing their dreams. Dream-chasing is not a frolic in a sun-drenched meadow. It's hard dangerous work. So most people play it safe.

"The good news is that by following some basic principles, you can construct a life resilient enough to handle chasing your dreams. Web of goals thinking can help. Imagine that you write down all of your goals and activities on little pieces of paper and then you dump them out on a table. They are all jumbled up. Is there any connection between your goals?"

"No," he says.

"Wrong," I say, "there *are* relationships between all of your goals. You just can't see them because they're all scattered in a heap. Start going through the pile of actions and goals like a puzzle. When you find two goals or actions that seem to have something to do with each other, put them close to each other and figure it out. Does one flow into the other? Are they in conflict with each other? Are the two actions both pointing towards the same goal? Make that connection clear, and then set that group aside and keep sifting through the pile. Always be looking for connections and relationships. At first you'll be connecting individual nodes, but eventually you'll start finding the connections between whole chunks of nodes. This is a good exercise for the next step, which is to sketch a web of goals. Let's do that."

Drawings Webs of Goals

"There are a lot of different ways to start drawing a web of goals. There isn't any one correct method. You should experiment around and find different ways that make sense to you. One way to start a web of goals sketch is to first write down some basic needs. Let's start small to keep this exercise manageable. What are two fundamental needs of yours?"

"Food," he says. "And shelter."

"And how do you meet those needs currently?" I ask, scribbling in the notebook.

"I rent an apartment and I pay for groceries and restaurants," he says.

"And alcohol and bars," I add.

"Alcohol isn't food," he protests.

"Splitting alcohol out into a different category is a waste of time. Think of 'food' as 'anything that goes down the hatch.' Keeps the sketches tidier, trust me. Okay, where do you get your money from?"

"My job," he says.

"So your current system for meeting your shelter and food needs is that you work a job, your money goes in your checking account, and you pay something like two thousand dollars a month just for shelter and food," I say, and show him my sketch.

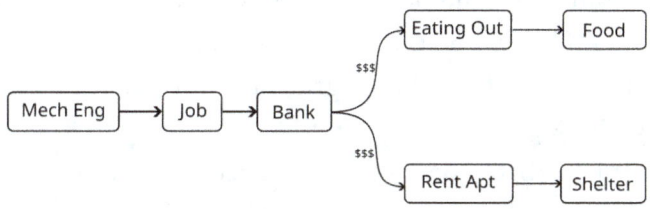

He looks at it and nods.

"Is this a web?" I ask.

"It is not," he replies.

"How can you tell?"

"It's linear," he says. "Just one skill, just one job, just one flow of money."

"That's right. Okay now let me sketch how I currently meet my needs for food and shelter. I've got a couple more skills than you do – 3d design and construction. I have at least three activities I do that bring in income: freelance design modeling, selling digital assets online, and off-grid design and build projects. With those flows of money I have investment accounts and a liquid savings account. I also have a tinyhouse, which means I don't pay rent, and my skills are such that I could worktrade for food and shelter almost anywhere in the world."

I show him the sketch and ask "Is this a web?"

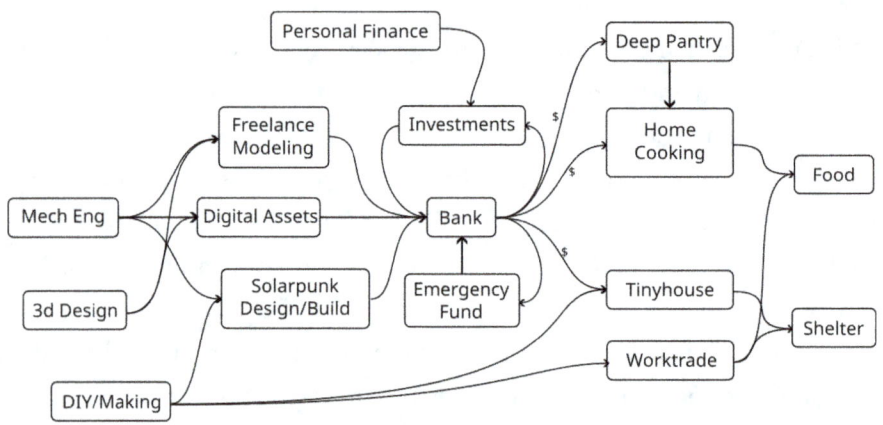

"It sort of looks like a complicated chain," he says.

I smile. "Sometimes the difference between a complicated chain and a web is subtle. What happens if I break my arm?"

"You won't be able to build off-grid stuff for people, so that income will go away," he says.

"But I'll still probably be able to freelance, and I've got digital assets passively generating income. So the off-grid builds node could get snipped but my system still functions fine. What if I got real sick and couldn't work for a while?"

He studies the sketch. "Well, you've still got investments and savings, so I assume you'd be fine not generating income for a while. Also, I guess the passive income would keep coming in."

I nod. "And what if I get real sick *and* my investments took a nose-dive?"

"You've still got savings," he says. "Of both money and stored food, in your deep pantry. It'd take a whole stack of misfortune for your system to not be able to meet your shelter and food needs."

"Yes. It's not impossible that enough bad stuff could happen to me that my system will fail, but it's unlikely. Even if all my assets got frozen or hyper-inflated, I have a pretty deep pantry so I've got months of food on hand to ride out short-duration emergencies. My system for meeting fundamental physiological needs is difficult to break. If I had a garden, or friends who garden, or knew how to hunt or forage, my system would be even more robust."

"I see how this works for basic needs, but what about things I want to do with my life, things that aren't necessarily physiological needs?" He asks.

"Take the same approach. Start with these desires, or desired effects, and see what activities connect to them, and think about the system from the perspective of how robust it is. Look out for nodes that would cause the whole system to fall apart if they got snipped. Look for multiple ways of fulfilling your desires. For example, you identified 'flow' as a desired outcome of mountain biking and climbing earlier, right? What else brings you flow?"

He thinks. "Writing, sometimes. And digital modeling. And having really deep conversations with friends, when it's really clicking."

I draw a sketch of writing, conversations, and 3d modeling connecting to a box labeled 'flow.'

"Do you think you like writing enough to try writing a book someday?" I ask.

He shrugs. "Sure, I'd like to try that."

"If you do like it, and keep at it, and get better, you might even be able to make a little money from selling books. So one possible side effect of writing is that you'd generate some income," I say, and draw this. "You enjoy 3d modeling and you're good at it. It's reasonable to assume you could earn income doing freelance 3d modeling if you tried. I know because I've done it. This would also generate income."

"Maybe, but I mean I have a job already—" he starts. I wave him off.

"We're just making connections and identifying potential relationships here, as a thought exercise. We're making a map in order to understand where we're at, not writing a set of instructions. Not yet, anyway. With the conversations you enjoy having, you could double down on that and start a podcast where you have conversations with interesting people."

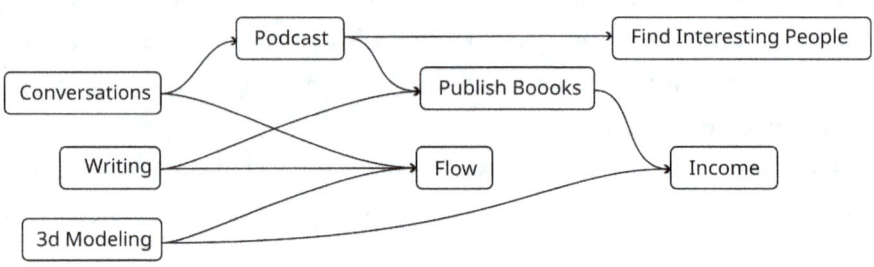

"What would that bring me?" he asks.

"Flow, for one. It'd help you develop your ideas more, for another, which would feed back into your writing. And you'd get to meet and have interesting conversations with more interesting people, some of whom you'd likely develop a longer relationship with. That, and your books, would act as a filter for attracting the kinds of people you want in your life." I look at the drawing. "Also, it'd help you get the word out about the books you might write, boosting income incidentally."

"Huh," he says, looking at the sketch.

"This is just a small map of a potential web of goals you might pursue. Like before, the value isn't in *the sketch*, the value is in *the activity of sketching*. It helps you to think in a particular way, to notice connections between things and to start to get an overall sense for the operation of your life system. It helps you start to intuitively notice things like single points of failures, friction, misaligned goals, unmet needs, needs you are meeting that you don't actually care about, and an alignment of values."

"How does this help me notice value alignment?" he asks.

"Roughly speaking, what is it that you find meaningful and

purposeful? What's the mission of your life?"

"Figuring out how to help humanity build successor cultures that suck less than the current global hegemon," he replies. I notice his answer is different now than it was when I first asked him.

"Presumably that's what you'd talk about on a podcast or write about in a book, right?"

"Ah, I see," he says. "So those activities are values-aligned, and 3d modeling office building mechanical systems isn't. So, I should talk and write and I shouldn't do the modeling thing?"

"Well, I bet there's more money in design modeling than writing and podcasting. Maybe you spin up a side hustle where you take on some modeling gigs for a few weeks a year and that pays your bills, freeing you to write and talk to your heart's content about subverting the hegemon without having to stress about making money or the optics of running advertising on your anti-consumerist podcast. You can add a node for "post-consumerism", which implies a very low cost of living, which would get you to financial independence earlier and contribute to your goal of subverting the hegemon, and free up more of your time to spend writing and talking since you could stop doing the modeling if you wanted."

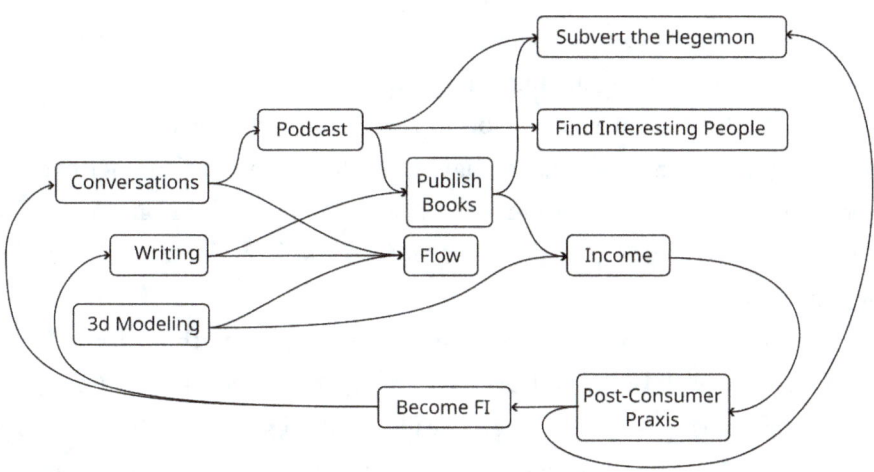

"Do you have a massive sketch of your entire web of goals

somewhere?" he asks.

"No, these sketches can get out of hand pretty quickly," I say. "I've never actually drawn up a full and complete web of goals of my whole life system with every detail. It's just a thinking aid. Again, the utility is in training yourself to think this way intuitively. The sketching exercises are just exercises, they are an activity that generate insight. I recommend you spend time with all these kinds of sketches for several weeks, and then revisit the exercises every couple of months and whenever you feel like you have a big decision to make.

"These sketches help you notice and identify single points of failure, friction, and misalignment in your life, and they help you think ahead so that you don't build those structures into your life. Make a habit of thinking through your decisions from this perspective and, over time, your life system will become more resilient, require fewer resources, and steadily increase in alignment with the things you want in life."

"So, let me see if I've got this," he says. "A big theme here is to pay attention to the relationships between parts of my life. Goals, behaviors, actions, and their effects. Just noticing all of the positive and negative effects of every action feels like a big step.

"Then, once I'm able to notice and start to see the patterns of my life as a system, I want to start making tweaks to the system, paying particular attention to multiple sources of income, resource buffers, and actions that are working against each other."

I nod. "Ideally you want to be doing things that move you towards multiple goals. This is similar to having multiple sources of income – if more than one action is moving you towards a goal, then one or two of those actions can get put on hold but you still maintain momentum towards that goal."

"If you organize your life in a web-like structure, with multiple flows of resources, and build buffers of critical resources like money and food, your life is going to be pretty resilient. And a resilient life system is about more than just not dying, it's about being able to take advantage of opportunities, being able to adapt to new circumstances. If your life system can *take a hit*, it also means your life system can *perform a pivot*.

You have a lot more freedom to try new things and experiment. Live somewhere else. Try a new venture. Pursue a new creative activity or relationship. You don't have to keep hammering away at one thing because there *is* no one critical activity that keeps your system going.

"When I think about my life, I'm often not thinking about the components of what I want to do. I'm thinking about the relationships between things, as I keep saying. I'm looking for sources of friction, and I'm looking for waste — outputs of nodes that leave my system. Permaculture is actually a great discipline to study for this. They're obsessed with closing loops, obtaining yields, and setting up niches and cycles in their systems that make best use of resource flows. I'm just trying to do the same thing, with my life."

He's nodding but his eyes look a bit glazed over.

"Once you get the hang of it you do it without effort. It does make it difficult to explain yourself, though. A lot of my decisions now are based on an intuitive sense of my web of goals. Something will feel *off* and so I'll clip it. Or vice versa, I'll sense a *leanness* somewhere and I'll add an activity that strengthens that area of my web. From the outside my actions can look erratic or nonsensical but internally it all checks out."

"Sounds like woo woo jedi stuff," he says.

I smile. "It is woo woo jedi stuff. But it is just a progression of simple principles and actions. Habituate a low burn rate to take pressure off your system. Develop broad skills to improve quality of life and decrease your dependence on money as a problem-solving tool. Build up resource buffers so your life can take a hit. Then, start thinking through the positive and negative effects of each of your actions, and what it is you're actually trying to achieve with your actions.

"Once that becomes automatic, start looking at the relationships between your actions. Notice when you're trying to go in two different directions at once. When that becomes automatic, start trying to map out *all* of your actions, goals, values, and needs — try to be able to see your life from outside of it, and notice if it's coherent and aligned as an entire composition. At this point things get hard to describe. You're more like a gardener. You will begin to let go of specific goals and projects and start arranging your life for maximum exposure to serendipity. You'll realize that the emergent opportunities that arise from the interaction of your life system and unfolding environment are more wonderful than anything you could dream up by yourself. It gets strange, but in a good way."

Further Reading

The very best thing to read next is Chapter Five of Jacob's book *Early Retirement Extreme*, "Strategy, tactics, and guiding principles."

Peter Limberg, interview with Jacob Lund Fisker, "Resolving the Meta-Crisis with Emergent Movement and Post-Consumerist Praxis w/ Jacob Lund Fisker," YouTube video, *The Stoa*,, September 2, 2021, https://youtu.be/0MGQgQZHx1Q?si=eCgTgJrGQw3-4LaZ

Wilson, E. O. (1998). *Consilience: The Unity of Knowledge*. Knopf.

Weinberg, Gerald M. (1975). *An Introduction to General Systems Thinking*. Dorset House.

Meadows, Donnella. (1999). *Leverage Points: Places to Intervene in a System*. The Sustainability Institute. https://donellameadows.org/archives/leverage-points-places-to-intervene-in-a-system/

9. A Predicament To Respond To

"The study of economic lift-off is well developed; touch-down has not been considered. There is an asymmetry here which would invite comment if applied to aviation."
— David Fleming, Lean Logic

"This still sounds so self-centered," he says. "I get that you're making yourself more resilient and free, but what about everyone else?"

I study the sidewalk for a while, forming my thoughts. "What's the purpose of it all?" I ask.

"The purpose of what?"

"What's so wrong with the world that you can't just leave it alone and live your own life in peace?"

"Our current system is insane," he says. "It's eating the world. The world will burn if we don't stop it. It's infantilizing. Consumerism feeds on human dignity and converts it into dependence and obedience."

"What is one word to describe the state this system is in?" I ask.

"One word…" he trails off.

"A term from ecology," I prompt.

"Oh. Overshoot. Human systems are in overshoot."

"Yes. Overshoot of what?" I say.

"Overshoot of the capacity of natural systems to supply humans with the resources our culture runs on. We're taking too much wood, too much minerals, too much topsoil, from the earth. We're dumping more pollutants into the air and the oceans than they are capable of absorbing without destabilizing the systems. We're eating at a faster rate that the world can regenerate—not just food but all the resources we use—and so we're depleting the capacity of the systems to generate resources. If the world were a factory, we're eating what the factory is producing but we're also eating the factory itself, the machines that make the food, so the amount of food the factory can produce decreases day after day. Which can only go on for so long, obviously."

"Obviously. And then what?"

He shrugs. "The inevitable consequence of overshoot is collapse. How that plays out exactly is not predictable. The future isn't clockwork. Will there be a big traumatic die-off with plagues and famines, or a long low-drama tapering of population levels because fertility rates drop a little lower than mortality? No one knows for sure. It's somewhere in between the two extreme possibilities."

"Yes," I say. "So human global systems are in overshoot, and without some magic appearance of resources or extra capacity of natural systems to absorb pollutants, some form of collapse is inevitable. With that in mind, what's the purpose of your work?"

"To prevent—" he stops. "Well. Not to prevent collapse. That's not possible. Collapse is part of the natural cycle of cultural evolution. To ease the collapse process?" He isn't asking me, he's phrasing it as a question so he can see how it sounds. "The more in overshoot we are, the worse the collapse is going to be. If the carrying capacity of the world is five, say, and we peak at a seven, that's an overshoot of two. Which isn't great. But if we kept on going up to ten, that'd be an overshoot of five. That'd be a lot worse."

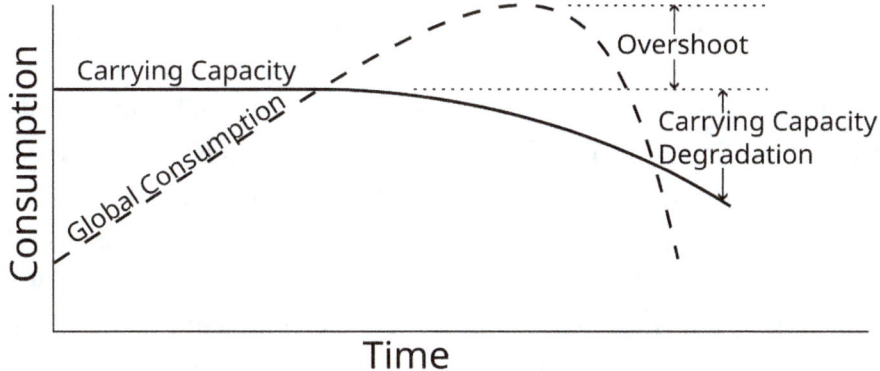

I nod. "The more in overshoot a system is, the steeper its correction will be. But with that being said, what most people get wrong about collapse is they assume it means some overnight global Mad Max apocalypse. Most people hear 'collapse' and think 'Armageddon', but they are not the same thing. Collapses aren't cliffs, where Monday you're watching a sports game live streaming on your phone while sitting in your self-driving electric vehicle and by Thursday you're hunting caribou in the ruins of downtown Manhattan with a bone spear. Every historical collapse we have information on took place over many decades and centuries. People living through collapse might not notice a huge difference between the beginning and end of their lives. Some people today don't even realize they're living in the early stages of an actively collapsing society."

"Sure, but also, no civilization has ever been global before," he says. "A dynamic of collapse is that, often, the society depletes their land base and so the complex society falls apart and people disperse and go somewhere else where the land base isn't depleted. There's nowhere else to go if the collapsing civilization is global."

I nod. "And no civilization has relied so heavily on nonrenewable resources to take its resource demand so high above the land base's actual renewable carrying capacity. You're right, we're in uncharted territory here. My point, though, is that most people think of collapse like a Hollywood movie, and so they either freak out and think the only thing to do is build a bunker and stockpile ammo or they dismiss the whole idea as wildly unrealistic conspiracy theory stuff.

"Even the people working in sustainability often think about it in a fuzzy way. They see collapse, which they haven't actually studied, as a defeat. They think collapse is a fast and huge process and represents total lack of control and total inability to influence the world around them. Collapse is game over. Collapse means 'we lost and we are losers.'"

I shake my head. "What most people mean when they say they want to save the world is that they want to save the 20th century way of life. They want to save professionalism, specialization, a society that runs on really dense and cheap sources of fuel, a highly financialized society, a society where its possible to become filthy rich. They want the world to operate the way it operated in the 20th century, mostly because it's all they know and also because the mythology of industrial consumer society insists that this is the best possible way to arrange society. And so their work implicitly is the pursuit of figuring out how make a fossil fuel civilization run on something other than fossil fuels but still operate basically the same way."

"The fallacy of the Great Swap," he says.

A Failure of Imagination

"Right," I say. "It's the idea that we can just swap out fossil fuels for windmills and solar panels and we'll be able to keep our 20th century lifestyles. Electric vehicles instead of gas guzzlers. Organic pasture raised instead of industrial grain-fed. Rooftop solar and smart grids instead of coal-powered. High speed rail instead of domestic flights. Everyone will work in the bright green economy and it'll be fine." I shake my head. "So few people understand how amazing fossil fuels are. How much energy is actually in a barrel of oil, how totally wildly unprecedented it is to have anything like that kind of energy density in a portable, stable fluid form, and how there just isn't anything like it on the horizon. Finding oil was like winning the lottery, and our civilization only works the way it does because of how incredible fossil fuels are. The idea of running our civilization on something else is like winning the lottery, living the high life for a few years, and planning on just winning the lottery again when the money runs out. It's a shit plan.

"The only two possible futures anyone can imagine is the Great Swap, which is biophysically impossible, or Mad Max apocalypse. It's maddening because no one seriously talks about a middle option, which is to figure out how to use way less energy—like, a tenth as much energy, per capita, at least—and have good lives while doing it. We're so baked into the paradigm of growth that we're blind to consider the strategy of just burning less energy.

"*Everyone* thinks this way. They're implicitly stuck in this illusion that they can buy their way to a sustainable lifestyle via ethical consumer choices, but there's no structural difference in their personal lives. It's greenwashed lifestyle design and it's a distraction. It's not so much a moral failing as a failure of imagination. It's an Overton window thing. There are so few examples of lifestyles and cultures that are structurally different."

"You seriously think we can save the world if a bunch of people adopt this post-consumer praxis idea?" he asks.

I blink at him. "You aren't hearing what I'm saying. Collapse is not a *problem to solve*. It is a *predicament to respond to*. Post-consumerism is a *response*. It won't stop the collapse of a civilization that runs on nonrenewable resources in massive overshoot of its land base. It won't save Netflix, Taco Bell, and ubiquitous car ownership. But it can at minimum help people have less bad lives. It can help rebuild human dignity. It gives people the tools they need to live good lives through this century, and to start building the durable cultures that *will* rise over the next few centuries.

"I don't know exactly what those durable cultures will look like, but I do have a sense. They'll be based on ecological principles because they'll have to be. The people of these cultures will have closer relationships with nature. The psychology of the culture will be one in which people don't think of the natural world as something apart from humanity. The cultures certainly won't run on the logic of consumer capitalism, because consumer capitalism is self-terminating on a finite planet.

111

Beginning the switch from consumerism to post-consumerism is something I can do now that is part of the broader work necessary to course-correct the trajectory of our species. It is far from all we have to do, but it is one of the obvious first steps. And it unlocks access to many more options for further personal and cultural development. In a sense, the consumer mindset is the first and most obvious cage to escape. So starting here makes a lot of sense.

"Most people, when they hear the word collapse, they think something like 'death', the flip of a switch. They assume collapse means that everything about society, all the good stuff we've built over the past few centuries, is just going to get dumped into a black hole somewhere and it's going to be gone forever, and if any humans remain it's going to be a life of horrific impoverished squalor.

"Of course if you think this is true, then the only moral thing to do is to fight to avert it. If collapse is the total end of everything good, then yeah. Fight it till your last breath. And anyone who suggests otherwise *is* a species traitor.

"The problem with this narrative is that it's based on a fantasy. Civilization collapse *isn't* a black hole. Collapse is a normal thing that all civilizations go through, and pretending that our civilization is different, like our civilization will never ever collapse, is ignorant. It's like devoting your life to never dying, instead of living a good life while you have one. It blinds people to the important work we've actually got in front of us.

"If you look back through history you see that there's a range of totality to collapse. A society flourishes, ascends in complexity, and then the costs of that complexity increase above some point and, typically, the society strips their landbase, and then there's a long descent. Everything doesn't just up and go full zombie apocalypse some random Tuesday.

"And the process of collapse isn't totally out of our control. We can make our own personal lives more collapse resilient, which is a good start, but also there's long term work to be done to make life better for future generations. A likely arc is that global industrial civilization is going to collapse, to transition from an industrial society to a de-

112

industrial society, over something like two to four hundred years. And successor cultures are going to grow out of that. Collapse is not an evenly distributed process. There are successor cultures being born right now even though we're in the early phases of collapse. There is almost certainly going to be *some* cultural continuity from now till 2400 and beyond."

The Work Starts Here

I pause. "And that means that there is meaningful and fulfilling work to do right now. There's work to do right now to make the collapse process less terrible, to begin to develop cultural and technological adaptations to a de-industrial transition.

"You said all this skill development stuff sounds self-centered. That is sort of the point. The work *starts* at the personal level, but then it spreads outwards to the group and community level. There's a reason they say to put your own oxygen mask on first. The no-brainer is to start experimenting with living off of way less energy and resources, and learn how to make a good life. Then figure out how to decouple from the flows of industrial civilization as much as you can, because those are going increasingly unstable.

"As you learn, you begin to integrate with other people. Despite starting at the personal scale, post-consumer praxis isn't a single-player game. Find friends and neighbors to play it with. Build strong web-like bonds of relationships. Reciprocal social bonds used to be normal but the logic of consumer society weakened and broke them. We don't need our neighbors anymore. Work to reverse this. It's part of the post-consumer education."

He's frowning, thinking. "Okay, but how inevitable is this model of collapse? In ecology, those graphs of collapse are looking at things like the population of coyotes and bunnies and clover or whatever, species that aren't capable of future planning. Bunnies just eat all the clover until they run out, they're not capable of building a critical resource forecast model and going oh hey guys, the clover is about to run out, maybe we should shag less otherwise a bunch of us are going to starve to death real soon."

"Sure."

"So that implies—well, it brings into question whether or not outright collapse is inevitable. Maybe humans as a species, as a global society, possess the capability of glide-pathing back to carrying capacity instead of collapsing down under it. Maybe we can do things ahead of time and bring us back to equilibrium with carrying capacity gently."

"Sure. It's theoretically possible I guess. But how do you think that's going?"

"I don't know," he says. "It's impossible to know. We won't know until the end."

"What end? There is no—never mind. Look, what you're doing seems to make sense. If we're in overshoot, we need to figure out how to bring our consumption down below carrying capacity. You're working on making buildings that use fewer resources than typical buildings. It checks out on first glance. Using fewer resource is the direction we need to go. Yes. But."

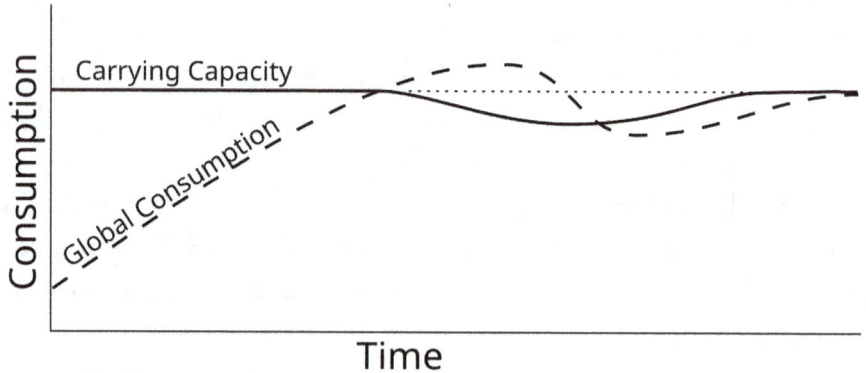

"But what?"

"But take another look, and what's the cause of the problem?" I say. "I mean, why are we in overshoot? Is it because all of a sudden a bunch of building designers got bad at their jobs, and started designing really inefficient buildings?"

"Well. No," he says. "We're in overshoot because of how the system is designed."

It's the Paradigm, Stupid

"The system is broken, man," I say, effecting an accent like a doped up hippy from the 60's. "Yeah, everyone knows that. What does that *mean*? Why are we in this mess in the first place?"

He blows out a breath, annoyed at me for poking fun at him. "The system is set up to grow or die. The logic of our economic systems means that growth is an imperative. We have no ability to grow a bit to an appropriate level and then stop growing and maintain—everything has to grow infinitely. And almost no one understands energy at all. No one understands how insanely unique fossil fuels are, how much energy is jammed into each gallon of the stuff and how extremely unlikely it is to find anything else that we'll be able to use instead."

"What's that called?" I ask.

"Energy blindness? Being bad at math? The failure of our education system?"

"No, I mean, that set of ideas about the growth imperative, how everyone accepts it as true, what kind of thing is it?"

"It's how everyone thinks, it's the myth of progress," he says. "It's the paradigm."

"It's the paradigm," I echo. "A colossus of an elephant sitting right in the middle of the living room that everyone has spent their whole lives ignoring so hard that they literally can't see it anymore. We have no idea how to live outside of the current paradigm. We have no idea what a non-growth-oriented world looks like. And if problem numero uno is that our paradigm is leading us off a cliff, then the Great Work of this century is to move to a different paradigm."

"This is what you couldn't handle, isn't it?" he asks.

"What do you mean?"

"Knowing the magnitude of the predicament, but working on a daily basis on projects still rooted in the existing paradigm. It drove you crazy."

I nod. "You and I have an abnormally high ability to live with cognitive dissonance. When most people experience a mismatch between their values and their actions, they change their values to conform to their actions. They justify their behavior via intellectual contortions. It's easier. I could never quite pull that off. But I didn't know exactly how to conform my actions to my beliefs, either, because there's almost no good guidance out there. There's no instruction manual for what to do about being a child of an ancient catastrophe. So I lived in a state of perpetual cognitive dissonance and it ground me up inside.

"You spend—I spent the next eight years struggling to figure out how to make my life make any kind of sense. I bounced between throwing myself at work, in near manic episodes of cranking on projects in the hope that I'd feel like I was making some kind of difference, to despair where I figured the most logical thing to do would be to blow my brains out with drugs and alcohol. Our brain is wired to thrash. We can't unsee the predicament. But we're not wired to totally numb out—we're wired just right to see the horror coming at our species and not be able to look away for long. And to feel like we've got to do something about it. To feel responsible.

"Unfortunately, we're also not wired smart enough to figure out what to do about it on our own. So we're stuck in a loop. You are one or two loops in by now. By 2020, I'd been through a dozen loops, seventeen, more, I don't know. It gets old, man."

Seeds of the Future

"But you broke out of the loop," he says.

"I broke out of the loop. That's why I'm here. I want to break you out of the loop too, but way earlier than I did. It doesn't have to take so long. Do I think a few pockets of post-consumers here and there are going to avert civilization collapse? Of course not. It's no longer about averting civilization collapse. It's about getting through it with something less insane on the other side of all this. And in times of trouble, people

116

tend not to come up with new ideas. They look around and use whatever ideas are handy. Me, and these small scattered pockets of post-consumers, we are one of those handy ideas.

"Post-consumerism isn't attractive to most people now. Consumerism is still a good deal for most people. It's still possible to get a cushy job sitting at a computer writing emails to get a paycheck that you can use to buy whatever nice food you want, pay for a comfortable apartment, drive around a comfortable car, and have comfortable vacations.

"But as time goes on, consumerism is going to work for fewer and fewer people. Post-consumerism is going to look more and more attractive. And those who went first will be able to help teach, support, and encourage those who come next. More and more people will shift away from consumerism and groups and communities of people will be more able to at least survive and maybe thrive though the process of civilization collapse. They'll be the seeds of the successor cultures that make it out of the next few centuries. That, broadly speaking, is what I'm doing."

"Collapse now, avoid the rush," he murmurs.

I nod. "At first that strategy sounds selfish, like you're turning your back on the world. Some people are. But other people, by simplifying their lives deliberately before being forced to by societal collapse, are playing the role of advance scouts, innovators, pioneers, or guinea pigs. They're showing that it's possible to live good, even better, lives on far less energy and resources, and they're making it easier for others to follow.

"You're fresh off of a phase of literal in-the-streets activism with Occupy Oakland and in the middle of a purpose-centered career focused on decarbonizing the built environment, so it makes sense that the work of building a desirable post-consumer lifestyle doesn't look like politically and socially engaged behavior to you. But it is. Figuring out how to live good lives on dramatically less energy throughput and with different social rules is necessary work that no think tank or government branch is going to do for us. We've got to do it for ourselves.

"Becoming a post-consumer isn't *all* we have to do. It's the *first* thing we have to do. If the paradigm needs to change, the first thing we need to do is exit the paradigm, imagine and invent and then inhabit new ones, and only from those perspectives will anything we do matters. Internalizing post-consumer praxis isn't about fixing the problem. Post-consumer praxis is about loading the cognitive software required to be able to respond to what is actually going on out there.

"It's one thing to say consumerism has to go. It's another thing to walk your talk and pull it off in your own life. So many people rant about the evils of consumerism but they still are madly trying to buy fulfillment, buy experiences, they're trying to buy the experience of having a good life as if that's something you can order next-day delivery. They're still trying to *buy* their exit from the consumer paradigm, which obviously is a tragic inability to see the system from outside the system.

"But when you're in a paradigm, it is difficult to see outside of it. And one of the things the paradigm does is convince everyone that there are only two options: the current paradigm, or brutal chaos and death. It implies that anyone who criticizes the current paradigm is an agent of death and chaos, is someone who is defeatist and wants to see the world burn and for people to go back to living in a state of disease and violence and early death and ignorance and all the rest.

"I believe that there are good lives to be lived in a different paradigm. This paradigm is self-terminating, and so despite all the wonderful things it's brought about in the world, we need to figure out how to shift to something else. My life is about exploring options for what that something else might be. I am absolutely not resigned to a future that sucks more than this present. I actually think that this present isn't as great as a lot of people like to think. We've got Netflix and insulin and everyone has access to most of the world's information, and those are wonderful things, but we're also headed off a cliff, causing a mass extinction event, and destabilizing the climate. Our mental health is not good. We could destroy everything in an afternoon by accident with our nuclear weapons. This paradigm is in grave danger of destroying everything beautiful that it has created. *I don't want those things to be destroyed.* I don't want to go 'back' to any previous epoch of human cultural evolution. I reject the whole notion that our options are forward or backwards. That's thinking from inside the myth of progress. I want us as a species to learn from the past one hundred, three hundred, ten thousand years, and figure out how to shift from a highly innovative and productive yet self-terminating system that seems intent on crushing human dignity, to a system that—"

I stop, and take a breath. "To a system that sucks less. We meant well with our old system, but it got away from us and is in danger of killing us all, of destroying the best parts of being human and the best parts of this planet. I want that to stop, but I don't *just* want that to stop, I want to be part of figuring out ways of being a human again. I want to live in a world where I don't have to work most of my hours in undignified, pointless labor just to be able to barely afford a shithole of an apartment that's made from toxic materials that poisons me and my family.

"I think part of the answer is to stop doubling down on the logic internal to this system. What seems like an obvious first step to me is to learn how to internalize the principles of post-consumer living at the scale of my own life, because that's something I can do right now. It happens to free up more of my time and agency, and makes me less fragile to disruptions. That's great, but it's almost a side effect, not the actual main goal. The main goal is to begin to learn how to think and act outside the dominant paradigm.

"Because I believe that the only way we get a better future, or a less horrible future than the one we're aimed at, is by acting in ways that we only can when we think outside the current paradigm. The personal scale, the household scale, is just the beginning. Getting my own house in order is arriving at the starting line. From there is the real work—the work of expanding this way of engaging with the world beyond the borders of my own life, finding other people who are doing the same, forming networks of people who are thinking outside of the dominant paradigm. This is the beginning of a project that is going to take hundreds of years.

"That's the point of all this. You've begun questioning the dominant paradigm, but you haven't gone very deep yet. You haven't questioned enough of it yet. You haven't yet questioned how much money you need to spend to have a good life. You haven't questioned why you feel compelled to work so many hours at such a high intensity level. And you haven't yet questioned the wisdom of living a life that is very fragile, very exposed to disruption."

When the Tide Goes Out

He frowns. "You haven't convinced me that the work I do decarbonizing the built environment is a waste of time."

I shake my head. "That's because I don't think it is a waste of time, necessarily. Your job is not what I have a problem with. I *do* have a problem with your fragility, how locked in you are to the consumer paradigm, and your inability to respond to serendipitous opportunities.

"I have a problem with you not having a large cash buffer. You should *always* have a large cash buffer so if something unexpected happens you won't panic, you can ride it out and make calm decisions.

"*And* I have a problem with your high burn rate. It's consumptive and therefore against our values, it makes it harder to save up a decent cash buffer, and it restricts what options you have to support you. It locks your mind into this paradigm where you *have* to have a roughly full time, roughly professional level salary.

"*And* I have a problem with you being really specialized. You don't know the first thing about growing a garden, brewing beer, first aid, decent cooking, or how to sew. You knew more about bike maintenance when you were nine. You wouldn't be able to install any of the stuff you spend all day designing on a computer. That is all a problem. It makes you reliant on being able to spend money to solve your problems, which is the definition of consumerism. It undoubtedly makes you a less effective designer of the kind of built environment we need, if you accept the idea that we've got to move past consumerism as a culture.

"*And* I have a problem with the fact that you use your sense of purpose to bury yourself in work, thrash your physical and mental health, and avoid dealing with your very normal human psychological dysfunctions. You can be engaged with making the world a better place *and* work on your own well-being and flourishing, which will lead to more positive experiences and more fully self-actualizing, but instead you just stuff all your problems in a closet and white-knuckle through the hard times.

"Add all these things up, and it means you're fragile without your job and without the whole consumer system continuing to function as it's supposed to. What do you do when the shelves go bare? When there's no one left to fix your bike for you? If something happens and your money is no good anymore? If AI design gets good enough to make a full set of engineering drawings from a concept report, and your specialized skills aren't worth anything anymore?"

He waves his hand dismissively. "That's so far off."

I shake my head. "Not as far as you think. My point is that you're using your job as an excuse to avoid dealing with your issues and as a result you will fail to flourish. Being fragile to disruption is one thing. But you're nerfing yourself. You're setting yourself up to not be the most kick-ass version of yourself, to fizzle, and to not fulfill your potential. I have a big fucking problem with that.

"So, fine, do what you want, but don't get caught with your pants down. The income you're making right now is freedom, and you're mostly flushing it away because unconsciously you think it's dirty. You're ashamed of it, or rather, you don't believe you deserve it, and so you ignore it, and that is indulgent of you. If you got a little more strategic with it you could buy yourself freedom of action. And once you have freedom of action, and once you internalize what it's like to be able to freely choose what to do with your time, and pursue any course of action that you deem the best fit for your talents and energy and stoke, then maybe you can do something that feels like it matters."

Further Reading

Fleming, David. (2016). *Lean Logic: A Dictionary for the Future and How to Survive It.* Chelsea Green Publishing.

Meadows, Donnella H. (1999) *Leverage Points: Places to Intervene in a System.* The Sustainability Institute.

Tainter, Joseph. (1990). *The Collapse of Complex Societies.* Cambridge University Press.

Diamond, Jared. (2011). *Collapse: How Societies Choose to Fail or Succeed: Revised Edition.* Penguin Books.

Meadows, Donella, et al. (2004). *Limits to Growth: The 30-Year Update.* Chelsea Green Publishing.

Ryan, Christopher. (2019). *Civilized to Death: The Price of Progress.* Simon and Schuster.

Greer, John Michael. (2015). *Collapse Now and Avoid the Rush: The Best of The Archdruid Report.* Founders House Publishing LLC.

Catton, William R. (1980). *Overshoot: The Ecological Basis of Revolutionary Change.* University of Illinois Press.

Murphy, Thomas W Jr. (2012) *Energy and Human Ambitions on a Finite Planet,* https://doi.org/10.21221/S2978-0-578-86717-5

Quinn, Daniel. (1992). *Ishmael: A Novel.* Random House Publishing Group.

Greer, John Michael. (2009). *The Ecotechnic Future: Envisioning a Post-Peak World.* New Society Publishers.

Callenbach, Ernest. (1975). *Ecotopia.* Banyan Tree Books.

Alexander, Samuel and Rutherford, Jonathon. (2020). *The Simpler Way: Collected Writings of Ted Trainer.* Simplicity Institute.

Bookchin, Murray. (2005). *The Ecology of Freedom: The Emergence and Dissolution of Hierarchy.* Cheshire Books.

Alexander, Samuel. (2017). *Art Against Empire: Toward an Aesthetics of Degrowth.* Simplicity Institute Publishing.

Greer, John Michael. (2016). *Retrotopia.* Founders House Publishing.

10. Don't Be A Stooge

"This still all sounds like it could be a rationalization for just doing whatever you want and ignoring the world's problems," he says. "How can you be sure you don't fall into the opposite trap, of being too self-indulgent?"

I blow out a breath and nod. "It is a danger. You're right to be concerned about it. You *can* get stuck in the details of getting your own house in order and sideline yourself. You need to be careful. But how can you be sure *you're* not being self-indulgent?"

"Huh?" he says, confused.

"You're so in love with your image, your idea of how much good you're doing," I say. "You *love* pulling all-nighters. You love staggering in the next morning barely able to see straight, knowing the stack of drawings is in good shape and the only reason is because of how late you worked. You think you care about saving the world? You sure about that? Are you sure you aren't just in love with the idea that you're a hero?"

"Hey, the work is important and no one else puts their hand up to make sure it goes out in good shape when it's a total dumpster fire and–"

"If no one knew that you worked so hard," I interrupt him, "if you were totally anonymous and just uploaded the files from an alias, would you still do what you do? Do you really do what you do because of the work? Or is it because of how you think it makes you look?"

"Who cares?" He shouts back in my face. It looks like his outburst surprises him. He wasn't expecting to yell at me. Excellent. We're getting somewhere. "Who cares if my motivations are selfish? I'm still actually showing up and *doing something*. Good for you that you retreated to the mountains and grow your own cilantro, but you've dropped out! You're not relevant anymore! What good are you doing anyone but yourself, huh?" He thumps his chest. "I'm working on a building that's going to have a *zero* net carbon footprint. I can't work on projects like that if I quit my job to fuck off into the woods to darn my goddamn socks!"

"They lay you off!" I roar.

Oh. Whoops. I hadn't meant to hit him with that yet. The cheap shot about the socks pissed me off.

He recoils. "What?"

Too late to back up now. "Keep doing what you're doing. Stay focused on all those super important projects that you're such a critical part of. They lay you off. You get the call on your thirty-fifth birthday."

This is so far from a possibility in the reality he lives in right now that it is difficult for him to wrap his head around it. In 2012 he can do no wrong at work. He's a golden boy.

A lot can happen in ten years.

"Why?" he asks in a small voice.

"You know how your dream right now is to do visualization work? I did that. In early 2016 I made a lateral career move to making design animations. It was fun, but it was all overhead non-billable work with a value proposition nearly impossible to prove. I knew it was a risk. I knew what might happen the next time the industry got tight because of economic conditions." I shrug. "Sure enough, I got a new boss who didn't see the value in what I was doing right when the economy got weird. It was a reasonable business decision. I'm not upset about it. When things get tight companies take a hard look at everyone who isn't directly and obviously contributing to the bottom line, and I didn't make the cut."

"I don't make the cut," he echoes. He sounds baffled.

I nod. "They cheaped out on my severance on a technicality, too, which kind of stung. It's not like I was entitled to it, but after twelve years of all the all-nighters, all the 80 hour weeks, the extracurricular work I put in in an attempt to make that place better, the risks I took, they saw an opportunity to pinch a couple pennies while getting rid of me and that's what they did. Because at the end no one gives a shit about what you did. What you gave."

I blow out a breath and shake my head. "I don't actually care about the money. At all. It just felt like a kick in the ass on the way out. The whole thing was a painful lesson to learn, but I'm glad it happened. I'm not mad at them. I'm upset with myself. For being a sucker. For getting my ego so wrapped up in something that was ultimately indifferent to my effort.

"This is the point. This is what I need you to understand. The lesson here isn't that they were mean to me. They weren't. They didn't treat me poorly. They treated me like an employee. *The point is that I was a sucker.* Naive. Idealistic and unrealistic. I treated the company like something more than a company. It was my source of validation."

He still looks shell shocked.

"I wish the story was that I quit on my own terms," I continue. "Getting laid off isn't a sexy story. But maybe a kick in the ass on the way out was just what I needed. To get humbled. If it's any consolation, by that time, I was happy to be set free. It was a gift. I didn't have to look for another job. I'd been cutting my costs and saving money for a year and a half by then so I had plenty of runway. I was going to make my life work for me, and figure out how to show up in the world on my own terms. I knew I was done with that world for good."

I turn and start walking again. He follows.

"Right now you're still full of energy. You're still convinced it's possible to make a difference designing buildings. But you've already got some doubts, some suspicions. Your doubts don't go away. They get worse. And you don't find an easier rhythm with work. You don't stabilize."

We walk together in silence a few paces.

"You'll start another project soon. The biggest you've ever done by far. Very high status. Very hip. You're going to be very excited about it. You're going to work so hard on it that you put someone *else* in the hospital."

He frowns. "How do I put someone in the hospital by working a lot?"

"You get sick. You were sleeping four to five hours a night, not eating well, really stressed. Most workdays were twelve to fourteen hours door to door. A flu took you down for a couple days, you got over it, but then your girlfriend caught it. The vomiting exacerbated an old back injury and the pain immobilized her. She couldn't move. Paramedics came to the apartment and took her to the hospital.

"She was in for a week. I stopped going to work and stayed with her almost the entire time. One day I was back at my apartment getting supplies and to take a shower. Catherine called out of the blue. She said she never heard from me and that I was finally in danger of being a bad friend."

He knows what this means. Catherine always insisted that my long silences and lack of initiative in our friendship were fine, that she'd always be there. For her to call me out on it meant that she had finally gotten sick of my shit.

"When I got off the phone I lost it, man. The stress of that week, the hospital, my job, everything, I put my head on the table and wailed like a baby for a solid five minutes. I didn't understood why at the time, but now, I think it's because that's when I realized that I was, in fact, capable of having an impact on the world. That's all we've ever wanted to do, right, since forever, is leave our mark on the world, leave some kind of trace that we existed. I wanted a sign that I mattered at all. And here, finally, was concrete evidence that I wasn't just an observer in the world, that I was making a difference." I'm silent for a few steps.

"But it was a *bad* difference," I bite the words out. It still stings, all these years later. "I was *hurting* people. Someone was in the hospital

126

because of me, and someone on the other side of the country was hurt because I'd been intermittently ghosting her for years because I had my head stuck so far up my own ass I couldn't tell what really mattered. A few months later that big sexy project got canceled. It just went away. My pain and the pain I put other people through meant nothing."

"Projects getting canceled is just part of the business," he says softly. I'm not sure if he's trying to console me or him.

"I know, but that one really took the wind out of your sails. Your capacity to believe in what you're doing gets slowly chipped away over the years. And then you get laid off with four day's severance, just to make sure you get the message. I honestly don't know if any of the projects made a difference. Maybe they did, maybe they didn't. It's not possible to know. In any case, by the end, you no longer *feel* that what you are doing matters, and you don't care."

I slow down and then stop to look at a tiny little patch of front yard garden. It's no more than ten feet by ten feet, but it is beautiful. Someone clearly loves that little patch of dirt. I've never made anything like it and my chest aches to look at it.

"You gave it too much. It never asked for that much. But you gave, and it took."

I turn and start walking again briskly.

"I worked my normal career for twelve years. And when I think back on it, it doesn't seem like I made a difference. Like I had any impact. Like it was going anywhere. It's possible I just did it all wrong. If I'd been able to do it with some stability, without just throwing myself at it, I could have stuck with it. I could have become a senior engineer in charge of really important projects, been responsible for projects that made a difference, maybe. Sure. But that's not what happened. I thrashed, burned hot, didn't actually accomplish much, fizzled out, and then got dumped.

"I remember how important my career felt, the work felt, when I was in it. Now that it's over, I almost never think about it. I also don't feel bad about it, I don't feel angry or sad. It's just an empty memory, like something that happened to someone else. Like I just showed up, moved some random things around, and then left, and nothing changed. I don't think it would have been any different anywhere else. There was nothing particularly wrong with that particular place. It was fine. The problem was me.

"The specifics don't matter. The point is that the traditional careerist approach is evidently not–" I look at him and smirk "–a good fit. For you, for me. It doesn't work out."

Further Reading

Schmidt, Jeff. (2000). *Disciplined Minds: A Critical Look at Salaried Professionals and the Soul-Battering System that Shapes Their Lives*. Rowman & Littlefield Publishers.

11. The Children of an Ancient Catastrophe

"So what am I supposed to do?" he asks. "If a career isn't a good fit for me... I mean, what, are you saying I should just learn how to live off of very little, reduce my footprint to something tiny, and then putter around? And be satisfied with minimizing the amount of harm I'm doing?"

I chuckle. "No, you aren't built for puttering. I tried that once and I wasn't very good at it. I don't know what you should do, to be honest. What I'm describing – a low burn rate, acquiring broad skills, internalizing systems thinking – it's all groundwork. It is the necessary, prerequisite work you must do to break out of the cage of modern industrial consumer society mindset, so that you can then get on to the important work, whatever work it is you're meant to do."

"How do I figure out what work I'm meant to do?" he asks.

"I don't know. I've only just gotten to the foot of that mountain myself. But I think I know how to get to the point where you can start working on answering that question."

He sighs. "Yes, right. Learn to live off of an equitable burn rate, become a polymath, think in systems. I got it."

"That's not all," I say. "Everything we've talked about so far is fairly tactical brass tacks kind of stuff. These lifestyle disciplines are intended to help you create a life that is *logistically* suited for pursuing your purpose, but that doesn't mean you'll be *psychologically, emotionally, or spiritually* suited for a life of purpose.

"Yes, you become financially independent so that you aren't beholden to a growth and profit-oriented organization for the resources you need, and you don't have to expend cognitive or physical attention on getting your basic needs met. You can put the entirety of your personal energy wherever you choose. You become broadly skilled and knowledgeable so you can think and execute across multiple disciplines. You internalize holistic systems modeling which is a much better map of reality than the old linear and mechanistic model. These attributes are just the cost of admission. Or, rather, they're the cost to claw your way out of the cage. But being logistically free is one thing, and being psychologically and spiritually suited for the task of building healthy successor cultures is another."

"What are you talking about?" he says.

"Our culture isn't very good at supporting the process of full human flourishing and development. This is partly because our culture has gone off the rails with the simple assumption that material affluence is the fundamental basis of human development, which is criminally simplistic. But it's mostly because, in the pursuit of global affluence, our culture has placed humans in service of the economy rather than the other way around. We humans are told in implicit and explicit ways that if we serve the economy well, then we belong. If we don't serve the economy well, we don't belong. This narrative has no place for the subtler desires and complexities of human flourishing. It has no or limited capacity for beauty, sensuality, spirituality, wisdom, play, individual self-expression outside of narrow confines. Huge swathes of human experience are treated like hobbies to be fit around the core function of economic and consumptive activity. As such, our socialized understanding of our selves is at odds with the deep-down desires and complexities that are common to all humans. We are given no guidance or support to deal with these complexities and so we are, most of us, fundamentally stunted, developmentally speaking. We're infantilized and pauperized, drowning in affluence and starving for personal and spiritual meaning. We're like well fed wild animals going insane in a zoo. We're all going crazy because some part of us knows there's a whole world of experience out there that we're intended to experience, but all we've got is this little comfortable pen of consumer society. We all crack up in different ways, but none of us are whole."

"Jesus," he mutters. "A bit melodramatic, don't you think?"

"I explained to you earlier how you get into consumer debt over the next several years. Doesn't that strike you as odd?" I say.

He frowns. "Yeah, what the hell? I'm a minimalism and anti-consumerist. I spent last year running around with a bunch of radical anti-capitalist activists. Going into consumer debt doesn't fit. What happened to you?"

The Dysfunction

"There's something in your life that overrides your values," I say. "There's an exploit in your brain. A flaw in your wiring. An old childhood survival tactic that subverts your ideals."

"What is it?" he asks.

"Why do you work so hard? Your salary certainly doesn't explain it. Nobody works this hard unless they've got an equity stake, and you don't. Why do you do it?"

He shrugs. "It's important work. I want to help fix things."

"You hurl yourself at projects as if the level of effort you expend is proportional to the level of self-worth you can claim. There's an element of guilt."

He flinches. "Guilt?"

"You've been horrified by how the world works ever since you learned about it. Racism, slavery, economic warfare, imperialism, genocide against indigenous people, the patriarchy, ecocide, the whole list, has filled you with horror from the beginning. And the fact that most of the people responsible for all that horror kind of look like you makes you feel like you have to try to kill yourself."

He stops walking. I stop too and turn to face him. There are goosebumps on his arms, I notice.

"You understand that it's cowardly to actually kill yourself, that it'd be selfishly performative to draw attention to yourself like that, but you think you can sneakily do it by working yourself to death, refusing to have nice things, and refusing to see after your own security and independence. You could just sink into oblivion, which is what you think you deserve. You think that if you refuse to consider your own wants and needs in the world, things like sleep and health and joy, then you won't be held responsible for what happened, that you'll get a pass."

"No," he says. "That's crazy."

"Don't lie to me. You are literally talking to yourself."

"I'm not suicidal."

"No, but you believe that you deserve to die," I say calmly. "The fact that you aren't dead confuses and terrifies you. You have a death wish." I look him in the eye, daring him to disagree. He looks down at the sidewalk.

"Where does it come from?" he asks.

"The guilt, you mean?" I ask.

He nods, then says "The hate."

"Hate always comes from fear. Fear of isolation. Your culture has failed you. It allowed you to become a human who thinks he doesn't deserve to live and isn't sure he wants to because of the sense of severe isolation and horror that simply being aware and sensitive in this world brings. Not everyone is sensitive or perceptive enough for these things to impact them at a conscious level. Most people jump on the hedonic treadmill, numb out the signals that all is not well with their culture, and sleep well enough at night. Other people can't look away from the train wreck happening beneath the surface of our world. That's you and me.

"And not only do we see the train wreck, we're not given any kind of story about what our place is, what our role is, in this whole narrative. The dominant culture gaslights us, tells us we're making stuff up, makes us doubt our own perception of the world. I spent a lot of time wondering if I was completely cracked up.

"Our culture lets us down. It stunts healthy human development. Humans are meant to flourish, to grow in wisdom, to be connected in a web of relationships with other humans as well as the rest of reality. But our culture isolates us from nature, from the rest of the world, gives us glowing screens to look at, and tells us that the path to happiness is same-day delivery and streaming entertainment. This is a big problem. It's a deeper problem than most of us are capable of recognizing, because it's been so long since any of us have encountered fully developed humans, humans who aren't fundamentally broken in any number of ways.

"Mature, developed cultures don't isolate people like this. They don't tell people lies about the meaning of their lives and then abandon them if they become economically nonviable. Our culture is fundamentally anti-human, anti-life. It doesn't support full-spectrum human flourishing. It's spiritually impoverished. The most sensitive individuals, the people who feel this impoverishment as a kind of psychological or spiritual pain are treated like cranks."

I shake my head. "Mature, healthy cultures all have a message of belonging baked into them somehow. A sense of belonging is one of the most fundamental human psychological needs. It's difficult to feel like you deserve to exist if your culture is indifferent to you and tells you that your most deeply felt truths are illusions. Doubly so if you get messages that you are insane because you see things other people don't.

"The result of all of this is that you became an adult incapable of robust self-validation. We can look ourselves in the mirror and say things like 'I belong here' and 'I am enough, just the way I am' but we don't believe it for a second. Different people come up with different methods of finding validation when they can't generate it themselves. Do you know what we do about that, how we cope with not feeling intrinsically worthy of existing?"

"We fix stuff," he murmurs.

I nod. "We fix stuff. Or we try to. Even better if we can find stuff that needs *rescuing*, which is like the crack cocaine version of fixing. Fixing and rescuing is how we keep our nose above the darkness. That's us, though. Other people respond differently to self-hatred and isolation, they get their validation fix in another way."

He thinks for a second. "Another strategy is just the inverse. Some people try to *get* fixed. Being rescued is evidence that they're worth something."

"Yeah. And who is motivated to actually get things working smoothly?"

"Huh? Both kinds of people are. People like us want things to be fixed–oh." He's silent for a minute. "No. We don't actually want things to be fixed. It's the activity of fixing that validates us. And the other kind of person doesn't actually want to be fixed either. Being rescued is how they get validated. When the validation hit wears off you need another one."

I nod. "People like us need the things around us to *remain* broken so we can keep fixing them. If we ran out of things to fix, we'd drown in the darkness. Fixing is treading water. The other kind of person wants to stay broken so they can keep being fixed. Imagine the implications if people like this ever met each other and, say, entered into intimate relationships with each other."

"Oh, hm," he says. "It becomes a feedback loop. The fixer and the broken one. They root in to each other."

I nod. "And what happens if one of the partners starts doing some internal work, goes to therapy, whatever, and starts to learn how to self-validate? Let's say the fixer starts to learn how to love himself without needing to fix his partner all the time."

"Well, he'll stop trying to fix her all the time, I guess."

"Right, and how will she react to that?"

"By fixing her less, he's withholding validation from her. She'll… I mean one way it can go is she'd amp it up. She'd act more broken, try to force him to fix her, to get her hit of validation."

"Yeah. And what if the broken one stops needing to be fixed?"

He's nodding. He's picked up how it works. "The fixer needs her to stay broken. He doesn't actually want her to *be* fixed. He'll insist she's still broken, still needs his help. God, these relationships must be almost

134

impossible to make healthy because it requires both partners to fix themselves at the same time at the same rate. Otherwise they drag each other back into old patterns."

I sigh. "And now you understand everything there is to know about the next eight years of my dating life."

He's frowning. "I don't see how it explains the last three years of *my* dating life…"

I shrug. "It's hard to see because that was mostly chaos, but it's in there. Your bald-faced lack of self-respect is more obvious. I can still recall several instances where any person with a shred of self-regard would have walked away on the spot. They're seared into my memory. You stuck around so long because deep down you didn't believe you deserved to be treated any better than dirt."

He winces.

"But there's a point of me digging into this stuff. First, I became aware of this dynamic about two or three years into your future. But it took me another six to sort it out, to stop behaving that way. I had to go all the way down to the core of who I am and learn how to love myself, to learn how to believe that it was okay that I exist. It wasn't until after I stopped throwing myself at a full time job, full time relationship, and a bunch of other stuff at the same time that I had the time and space to devote to myself. Do you see? This is another reason why autonomy is so important. I didn't have the time and space available to do the internal work necessary until I'd stripped most things out of my life. I first had to remove my supply of fixer validation hits, to basically put myself through fixer rehab and detox, in order to build a life of self love and self validation."

"I see why you had to be not in a relationship to fix this, but I don't see why you had to leave full time work," he says. "Surely there's enough hours in the day, even if working full time, to do whatever DIY therapy you did?"

"What makes you think work isn't a relationship?" I ask.

"What?"

"You get into fixer-fixee relationships with women," I explain. "And

135

you get into fixer-fixee relationships with work, too."

"I don't get it," he says. "I'm a mechanical engineer. My job is to solve problems."

"Sure, but what is it that you joke your role is at work?"

"I'm the dumpster fire putter-outter," he says.

"Yeah," I say. "Projects get into dire straights and they need a rescue. Who do they call? They call the guy who always says yes, who will work nights and weekends without being asked, the guy who is creepily cheerful about being asked to fix things that are real broke and stays up all night to do so without complaining. It's a brilliant strategy you've got. In your home life you get validation hits from a partner who accepts your fixes and rescues because they validate her. During the day, you get constant validation hits from colleagues who appreciate you cleaning up messes. So much juicy validation. Why do you think all you do is work and spend time with your partner, and nothing seems to go anywhere? Why your life feels like it's a loop?

"It's because you optimize your life for the highest frequency of the best, highest grade of validation hits. You get validation hits every couple of hours you are awake. It doesn't get any better than that. Your own interests and dreams and desires can't get you validation hits like a real nice hot dumpster fire at work. So you work ten, twelve, fourteen hours a day, and you come home and try to fix and rescue there too. And subconsciously you do everything in your power to make sure that everything around you is broken and stays broken. Your relationship with women and your relationship with work is the same. They're both validation delivery mechanisms. This is how you sabotage your own life."

He shakes his head. "I hear you, but I also don't get it. I don't *want* that. I want to be effective. I want—I truly want—whoever I'm dating to be the best version of themselves. I truly want the company to be the best it can be, so it can make a positive impact in the world. I want to have highly functional relationships, and I want to live in a world that sucks less. And I have ideas for things I want to do myself, my own dreams and visions. It's all I think about. You're saying the opposite."

"I'm not. Both are true. The top level of you wants everything to *be* fixed. A deeper level of you wants everything to be *broken* so you can suck validation hits off of it. Here, look," I say, and stop walking. "Lay down."

The Void

"What, here? On the sidewalk?"

I spot a front yard that has a thick layer of wood chip mulch on it. "Here. Lay down and close your eyes."

He squints at me. "This is weird."

"I know, it's fine. Trust me," I say. "I wouldn't hurt you."

A shadow ripples over his face and he looks away quickly. He finds a spot in between clumps of tall grass and stretches out. I sit cross-legged next to him. The mulch is moist from the rain but not waterlogged. It actually feels a little warm, and it's soft. It's nice. With a good blanket I could fall asleep here.

"Close your eyes and take slow, deep breaths," I say. "Relax. Let go of everything we've been talking about. Just focus on your breathe." I talk him through a few minutes of settling into a relaxed state.

"Imagine you are dating a woman who is capable and independent. Don't imagine a perfect person, just imagine a person who possesses a strong sense of self worth and is able to handle everything in her life. She likes you, but she'd be fine on her own without you. She spends time with you because she enjoys spending time with you. If you told her you needed to break up with her, she'd be sad but she'd accept it and move on and be fine.

"Now imagine that you work at a company where all the projects go smoothly. Where everyone is competent and rarely screws up, but when they do they fix their mistakes themselves. Imagine a workplace that is well organized, calm, professional, and executes well. Imagine that they gave you thorough training when you were hired, and made their expectations clear. You go to work at a place that accepts your effort, but doesn't need you because it's a well run organization, and you go home to a partner who loves you but is obviously fine without you.

Imagine it. Visualize it. How does it feel?"

His face goes slack as he drifts into his imagination. After a moment I see the ghost of a smile rise. "I mean, it feels pretty nice."

"Stay with it," I say. "Go deeper. Drop into it. Let go of thinking about it, and instead just hold the visualization of that life and let feelings arise. Don't *think* about what it's *supposed* to feel like. Let go and feel what naturally arises."

He shrugs and takes more deep breaths. The smile fades to a blank expression. A minute passes. Lines form on his forehead. Another minute.

His upper right lip twitches. The muscles in his neck constrict and his face pulls inward like he bit into something sour, and then his whole upper lip scrunches up like he's smelled something rotten. Yep. There it is. His lips part like he's about to retch.

"That's enough," I say. "Open your eyes."

He doesn't react. His face continues to twist.

"Hey," I raise my voice. "Snap out of it."

He starts to curl into a fetal position like a poked rollie-pollie. Oh, hell. He fell in. He can't hear me.

I reach out and roughly shove him on the shoulder. "Wake up!" His eyes pop open and he rolls onto his side, making a noise halfway between a cough and a choke.

"What the fuck was that?" he gasps.

"That," I say with a sad smile, "was the void. Don't you recognize it?"

"I thought I was done with that," he mutters.

"You developed a *coping mechanism* for that. You buried it. Our brains will lie to us all day long, but our bodies know what's up. We just have to shut up long enough to listen, and they'll tell us the truth about ourselves."

"But I was thinking of something *nice*," he protests. "What the hell?"

"Nice to your conscious self," I explain. "I asked you to imagine a world where you are getting no external signals that you are worthy of love. It's a world where you've hurled yourself into the darkness: completely alone and completely worthless. It's more horrible to your subconscious than death. What did it feel like? In your body?"

"A clenching in my gut, and like there were ants running underneath my skin. The darkness felt thick enough to bite into. It felt like I want to collapse into a hole… and like I also want to run, and to feel pain. It made me want to feel physical pain, to block out *that*."

It's been a long time since I felt it myself, but I remember the sensation well. "Yeah. Odd, right? It's not just that you seek out things that need to be fixed, but you have an extreme aversion to things that don't need you. A world that doesn't need you is so terrible that you'd rather feel physical pain. You reject that reality at a physiological level. You zero in on broken things and pursue them relentlessly."

"I don't *want* that," he says again, quietly. I know he's not talking to me.

"This is why you get laid off, by the way."

He looks at me sharply. "What?"

The Saboteur

"You were a good little dumpster fire putter-outter. Your value was clear. But as I first began to work on this part of myself, I tried to move in the direction of my dreams. My vision. What *I* wanted to do in the world. I tried to convince myself that I was ready to self-validate, even though I didn't realize that's what I was doing. I negotiated a new role for myself at work and I stopped putting out dumpster fires. Instead I was supposed to be focused on making things, creative things, the visualization work."

"Oh," he says. "You cut off your supply of validation dope at work."

I nod. "Before I was ready, yes. Until that point, I ran on external validation hits from fixing and rescuing—that was my motivation, my fuel, and also my creative spark. It's what got me going. When I shifted to generative work…" I shrug. "No more fuel. I think my idea for what I wanted to do was good. But to pull it off I needed to be able to *push* it, you know? I needed to be able to hustle and drive and dump a lot of energy into it, and I had to believe in myself. But I wasn't ready to do that. I was in validation withdrawal. So my work was… not as good as it needed to be. Which made me doubt myself even more. Like I said, laying me off when the economy got sketchy was the right decision on their part. I'd have done the same."

"So I've got to be careful about how I approach this," he says.

"Yes, you do," I say. "Going off the validation dope cold turkey might not be the right move, not without a support system in place to catch you. But I'll leave the planning to you, now that you understand what you're up against. I trust you to build a strategy for it. We have to talk about another consequence of this dysfunction now."

He looks at me and arches an eyebrow.

"You're a person who needs to be around broken stuff, and you need that stuff to stay more or less broken even though you spend all your time trying to fix it." I lean forward to emphasize my next sentence. "And your chosen life's work is the Metacrisis, the Predicament. The wickedly complex brokenness of the whole world. Climate destabilization plus resource scarcity plus environmental toxicity plus economic injustice plus blah, blah, blah."

His eyes widen. It takes a lot to get me to display actual surprise like this. I have a pretty good poker face. But this hits him like a wave he had his back to.

"How interesting, yeah?" I press on. "You're a person who needs an infinite supply of validation from the activity of fixing and rescuing, and your chosen obsession is to fix the biggest, most complex, most unfixable brokenness in the world. And you need your broken things to stay broke." I make a tsk-ing noise. "I wonder what the potential ramifications of this dynamic are?"

I stand and put my hand out. He takes it and I haul him to his feet. We brush bits of mulch off our clothes and start walking again. He looks dazed, his movements half conscious.

"This is why I say it's hard to know if what you're doing, the things *you specifically* are doing, is making a positive impact in the world. Decarbonizing the built environment is obviously a worthy enterprise. It's good that people are working on it. But you have an unhealthy relationship with broken things. You sabotage your own dreams, and maybe you sabotage the very things you're theoretically trying to fix. The way you are now, you might be poison to any healthy culture you try to contribute to." I shrug. "The whole thing is a mess the way it is. It's best to resolve this whole internal business, make yourself whole."

"But how do I even start that?" he says.

"For you, read Bill Plotkin's book *Nature and the Human Soul* for a starting point," I say. "It'll guide you from there."

"Wait, though," he says. "I still don't see how all this leads to me getting into consumer debt, which is how we started talking about this in the first place."

"That comes from your relationships. You have a pathological need to be close to people you get off on trying to fix. What's the easiest way to fix things when you spend a lot of time at work and make decent money?"

"Oh. Money," he says. "Spending money to solve problems. Consumerism."

I nod. "It's also an easy way to control people, to keep them close. Make them dependent on you and your financial fixes. You don't blow money on toys for yourself because you don't think you deserve nice things. You blow your money maintaining dysfunctional relationships. It looks like you're being a provider, but it's coming from a corrupted motivation. Your providence is an unconscious tactic to control, to keep your source of validation hits close. Nice apartments, nice vacations, nice food, nice gear, nice beer. And the whole time your anti-consumerist values are in conflict with your actions. Your cognitive dissonance twists you up inside like a wet rag, adding fuel to your fire of self-hatred."

"What a mess," he says. From the corner of my eye I can tell he's looking at me. I don't meet his gaze because I don't want to see any pity in it. I don't want that memory in my head.

"But you fixed yourself?" he presses. "You're over this?"

I consider my words before responding. "I have put more effort into this than anything else in my life. I consider the project of flipping my orientation from fear and hate to love, and building an authentic sense that I deserve to exist, to be the hardest thing I've ever done, and the thing I'm most proud of. I had to sacrifice a lot. I am not done, and I don't think I'll ever be done. But I've come a long, long way."

"Not a weekend seminar sort of fix, then," he says.

I laugh. "I'm afraid not. It's not just a matter of re-soldering some neural wiring and being done with it. This is why autonomy is so important for you. This is why having the freedom to wander off into the mountains if you want is important. I had to get away from it all, and I guess you will too. The greatest progress I made was when I cut off my supply, when I isolated myself from it for a time. I *had* to get away from it to be able to build a foundation for myself.

"If you want to have any hope of making a positive impact on the world, if you want to be able to participate effectively in the project of healing the world, if you want to have a real and authentic relationship with yourself, you've got to do this. You've got to learn to believe in yourself and you've got to figure out how to stop trying to control broken things.

"It is fundamentally not enough to free yourself. You've got to become worthy of contributing to the successor cultures you want to be a part of. It isn't fair that you've got to figure out how to do that as an adult. Your culture should have done that for you. But that's the hand we've been dealt, all of us, for generations. We're trying to bootstrap a healthy culture out of the ruins of a toxic and terminally flawed one. Your options are to wallow in self-pity about that, or to roll your sleeves up and get to work. Choice is yours."

Further Reading

Braitman, Laurel. (2014). *Animal Madness: How Anxious Dogs, Compulsive Parrots, and Elephants in Recovery Help Us Understand Ourselves*. Simon and Schuster.

Plotkin, Bill. (2007). *Nature and the Human Soul: Cultivating Wholeness and Community in a Fragmented World*. New World Library.

Plotkin, Bill. (2013). *Wild Mind: A Field Guide to the Human Psyche*, New World Library.

Mate, Gabor and Mate, Daniel. (2022). *The Myth of Normal: Trauma, Illness, and Healing in a Toxic Culture*. Penguin Random House Higher Education.

Beattie, Melody. (2022). *Codependent No More: How to Stop Controlling Others and Start Caring for Yourself (Revised Edition)*. Spiegel & Grau.

12. The Door Of Your Cage Hangs Open

The real damage is done by those millions who want to "survive." ...those people who roll up their spirits into tiny little balls so as to be safe. Safe? From what? Life is always on the edge of death; narrow streets lead to the same place as wide avenues, and a little candle burns itself out just like a flaming torch does. I choose my own way to burn.
— *Sophie Scholl*

I look up at the stars to the north. "Okay. It's time. This is where I'll go back," I say.

"Random spot," he mutters. We're at the side of the road, overlooking the steep north facing slope into Tilden Park. There are a dozen houses on the slope. Beyond, to the north, it's acres and acres of rolling hills with gum trees and coast oaks.

I smile. "It's a good place." I remember years ago a walk here, only a few months into his future. I saw the sky breathe then, and I also saw a festering darkness in the sky that I chose to not fall into. My ability to look away gave me strength I've carried with me ever since. I remember seeing the warm light from the windows of these houses in the dark and understanding what my purpose was. I remember a kiss that I could see from the inside out. I remember a gentle kindness that held the hard things inside me for a moment.

It's a good place.

"I still don't get why more people aren't doing this kind of thing," he says.

I nod and pause, thinking. "What is the most efficient design for a prison?"

"What, like the panopticon?"

"No, nothing architecturally clever, just think about prisons generally. The point is to keep prisoners inside the prison. What's the most efficient setup in terms of how much it costs in labor, money, and materials to keep the prisoners inside?"

He thinks for a few steps. "Well, building your prison on a remote island or in the middle of the desert might be a way to do it. There's no point in escaping over the walls because you'll die in the ocean or the desert. You can save money on walls, razor wire, and guards."

"That's a good idea. But building and keeping a prison supplied in the desert or an island would be expensive. So you can go further with that idea, make it even more efficient."

"Okay… build the walls tall so prisoners can't see out, and then just tell them they're in the middle of a desert or on an island. If you can convince them that escape is doomed, they won't even try. You could build your prison in the Garden of Eden but it doesn't matter so long as your propaganda is on point."

"Nice, yes," I say. "It's not necessary to *have* scary monsters if you can get people to *believe* scary monsters are real. Okay, our efficient prison design is almost complete. There's one more thing you can do to make it so it runs itself. What is it?"

He knows where I'm going with this.

"Make it really nice. Have good food and entertainment. Make it not look like a prison. Eventually the prisoners will forget they're in a prison. Not only will they be afraid of the world outside the prison walls, they can't imagine why they'd want to leave in the first place."

"They can't imagine why they'd want to leave in the first place," I say. "You no longer need to buy razor wire, hire guards, or anything else.

The perfect prison."

"But, I mean, it's not like anyone actually *designed* the world to imprison people. There's no conspiracy of evil elite masterminds chuckling over their brilliant plan to keep everyone enslaved and stupid," he inflects his tone at the end like a question. He wants to know if there's information to the contrary in the future. I give him a hard serious look for a solid few seconds, just to mess with him.

"No, I think you're right," I admit. "At least, not overtly like that. I don't believe there's anyone in the system who isn't a prisoner. Even the elites. They just have really nice cells and lots of power over the other prisoners. They still die choking on the cold ashes of what their lives could have been. I don't think it's very useful to imagine that there are evil cabals of elites messing with people."

I pause and think for a second. "I mean, we should still definitely take power from the elites and break their stuff, because fuck them, but if we want to make a system that sucks less we need to understand as accurately as possible what led us to this predicament. It's important to understand how alluring the illusion of the current arrangement is, how there are forces at play to maintain that illusion, that promise of a shiny and easy life that is so enticing to people. Once you scratch away at the illusion enough, though, it loses its power."

"Isn't that a letdown?" he asks. "Or just a total punch in the gut? To realize that everything is unraveling, that the shiny illusion is just an illusion, that the real world is a dark place?"

"Oh, no," I say. "Just the opposite. Once you see the truth, you are free to realize that this moment in history is truly, deeply amazing."

He raises his eyebrow at me. "How so?"

"The hugest, grandest system humans have ever come up with is running up against the biophysical and thermodynamic limits of the planet. Yes, it's a train wreck, but it's happening slow enough that we can observe, learn, plan, build, and respond to what's happening. For the first time ever humans are going to—as a global consciousness—understand the biosphere in a way that you only understand when you break things that happen to be responsible for the food you eat, the water you drink, and the air you breathe. What is culture going to be like in two or three generations? Will there be crazy taboos against digging holes in the ground, for any reason, even shallow ones, like to bury dead people, because that is the direction oil came from? Who knows! But either way, whoa! For the rest of your life every year is going to be the most interesting year in the history of our species."

"What the hell?" he says. "People are dying and suffering, and it's going to get way worse, and you're gloating about it being *interesting?*"

"Are you offended that I am not performatively affecting the proper tone of grief and outrage?" I shrug. "Look, I'm dedicated to not making it any worse as a baseline, and doing what I can to actively make it suck less for people in whatever way I can. But I am under no obligation to curl into a morose ball of grief for the rest of my life about it. Humans aren't built to be able to handle or understand global tragedy at the scale of what's coming. That's another thing it's not worth maintaining a shame narrative over. Look, the way things are going, a plausible end of life scenario for me is to get killed in a heat index event, or starve during a famine, or a freak storm, or by some weird disease that may or may not have been made in some nerd's mom's basement, or in a wildfire. Or some warboy will take me out. Hard to say. And that'll probably really suck. But as a percentage of my life, that experience will be pretty minor and death comes for us all anyway, one way or another."

"Jesus, man," he says. "How do you not care about how you—"

"And do what with that caring?" I interrupt him. "Megaviolence is baked into the cake we've had in the oven for the past three centuries. That's our world now. I could devote my life to the project of dying peacefully in bed of old age, but that would take a lot of effort, and it's kind of a stupid goal. I'd have to build a bunker, or hide really deep out in the mountains somewhere, I guess, but I just don't care enough about dying comfortably to make that my life's work. The person I am now doesn't want to get to the end of his life and realize that he spent it trying not to die instead of living."

He blinks rapidly. I'm throwing a lot at him. He hasn't spent much time thinking about dying violently yet.

"And that's really what I'm getting at. You and I, and everyone else alive now, have a profound opportunity to live lives of meaning because of what's happening. The world is passing through a narrows right now. Who cares about your end of life plan? About trying to live comfortably? I want to help. I want to participate in this beautiful mess, not sit on the sidelines. I want to build something that I decide means something in this moment of time. I can't do that if I let myself get trapped by the hedonic treadmill, consumer ideology, hyperspecialization, linear thinking, and my own psychological dysfunctions. I need to craft myself into an agent that can move freely through this moment in history if I'm to have any hope of building something beautiful."

"Does it actually matter?" he asks.

"In a cosmic sense? No, of course not," I say. "But I don't care. I decide it matters, and that's enough for me. We humans built a machine, the world system, to serve us but it got out of hand and now *we* serve *it*. It's stuck in a positive feedback loop and it's going to grow and grow and eat and eat until it runs out of cheap resources, the maintenance costs of complexity force widespread simplification, and it unravels itself. Does that actually matter? Nah, not really. But I don't like it, and so changing this in some small way, whatever I'm capable of, is what I'm about.

"The most important first step is to decouple our minds, our souls, our daily lives from the machine. To free ourselves from the prison that we all just accept, the prison of not even being able to imagine any other way of running a society, the prison of not being able to imagine other ways to be human. This is why I'm not against any specific thing you're doing in your life right now. I am against you remaining in a comfortable prison and not even realizing the staggering horrific beauty of the real world outside the walls. I don't want you to quit your job. I don't care about your job at all. I want you to quit being a prisoner of the machine. I want you to take control of your life and live in awe and to be in possession of your own self sovereignty.

"If you do that, if you get to that place of awareness of yourself and the world, and you are able to love yourself enough to let yourself *be* yourself in the world…" I shrug. "Then everything else is just details and destiny."

I look out to the east. The sky is just starting to lighten there. "I really do have to go now, though. Sorry I kept you up all night. It's going to be rough getting that drawing set out on no sleep."

"I think…" he starts to say, also looking at the dawn horizon. "I think I'll call in sick today." He looks at me and smiles. "I've got some things to think about this weekend."

I smile back at him. "Take care, self."

"You too. Hey," he says.

I look at him.

"Thanks."

Gratitude

Thank you Zola, Ivan, Bryan, Will, Meghan, Daylen, and Jetze.

Thank you Laura, Jack, Caryn, and Cole.

Thank you Cody, Duncan, Kevin, Susan, Emily, and Matt.

Thank you Jacob.

Thank you everyone who engaged in my journal or in conversation. It'd take another book to list all of you.